PAPERBOY

STEVE WHYSALL

COPYRIGHT

Copyright © 2025 by Steve Whysall

All rights reserved.

No part of this book may be reproduced in any form or by any electronic or mechanical means, including information storage and retrieval systems, without written permission from the author, except for the use of brief quotations in a book review.

ISBN 978-1-0693021-2-0

DEDICATION

For Loraine

This book would not have been possible without the love and support of my wife, Loraine, who has been my loyal and trusted advisor throughout the entire project. She is the reason I was able to sustain my energy and enthusiasm throughout.

INTRODUCTION

Paperboy is a work of fiction inspired by my first four years as a reporter working from 1968 to 1972 for the Ilkeston Advertiser and Erewash Valley News in Derbyshire, England.

For the purpose of this story, all names and places have been changed. I cannot rely entirely on my memory, and I have no wish to give offence to any who might think they are depicted in the book. Therefore, characters and events in the story are entirely fictitious. Any similarity between them and actual characters or events is entirely coincidental.

The primary purpose of this book is to amuse and entertain my grandchildren. I have told them about my early life and adventures as a junior reporter in Derbyshire.

It was a wonderful, quirky, eventful, fun-filled time that shaped many of my thoughts and interests today.

In 1975, Loraine and I met and married in London. We decided to make our home in Canada, where we have lived in Burnaby, British Columbia, for the past 46 years.

* * *

ABOUT THE AUTHOR

Steve Whysall is an English-born writer who was the garden columnist for The Vancouver Sun in Vancouver, British Columbia, Canada, for 26 years.

He has been married to Loraine since 1975, and they live in Burnaby, B.C. They have three children and seven grandchildren.

Steve is the author of four bestselling gardening books, 100 Best Plants for Coastal Gardens, 100 Best Plants for Ontario Gardens, The Blooming Great Gardening Book and Best Plant Picks.

In addition to writing books, Steve has led more than 30 garden tours to various parts of the world, including England, Ireland, Scotland, France, Italy, Spain, Germany, Czechia, Morocco, Japan, China, South Africa, the Netherlands, Myanmar, Singapore, Hong Kong, and Croatia.

Steve loves working in his English-style garden and also enjoys travelling, listening to music, visiting art galleries, origami, watching soccer, swimming, and going for walks, especially when they include stopping at an English pub.

* * *

CHAPTER ONE
BUS

On that Thursday afternoon in October 1968, the bus ride from Nottingham to Chesterton took less than half an hour.

As I stepped onto the platform of the bus and made my way upstairs to the top deck, I recited my own oath of optimism, part Cub Scouts, part John Lennon.

"I, Timothy John Malcolm, promise to do my best, to do my duty to God and the Queen. Amo amat amass; Amonk amink a minibus, Amarmylaidie Moon, Amikky mendip multiplus Amighty midgey spoon. Onward, Onward, Onward."

Being first to board the bus, I had my pick of seats. I took the best one; upstairs, right at the front, directly above the driver's cab. Words on the panelling in front of me said, "Please don't stamp your feet."

From this prime spot, I had a clear view, through large windows, of the road ahead as it twisted and turned and rolled out ahead of me.

It was a constantly changing scene as the bus trundled, groaned, and gear-crunched its way up hills and rushed down the other side, racing along like a fleeing prisoner.

Every now and then, it shuddered to a jerky, jolting, ill-tempered stop to let passengers off or pick up new ones.

Then came the predictable, neck-jarring, lurch forward as it pressed on, slowly grinding through gears to rebuild momentum.

I stared out the window in a blissful, trance-like state of half-consciousness. My eyes scanned the streetscape as it unfolded in front of me, a constantly changing scene of everyday life.

For a moment, I imagined I was in a painting, perhaps a Bruegel, only the people I was looking at were not 16th-century peasants at play, but penniless town dwellers, just as busy and engaging as their historic counterparts and just as weather-beaten and hapless.

In a blue-and-white striped apron, I saw a butcher, using a rough brush to scrub the front steps of his shop. He paused now and then to wave to people across the street.

A young, thin, pale-faced woman in a headscarf cranked the door handle of a hardware shop, but the shop was locked and bolted, secure as a fortress. A hard-to-miss CLOSED sign hung in the window. I imagined she was there to ask for her money back. I knew she didn't stand a chance.

The bus rushed past a pub. The name appeared and disappeared in a flash. What was it? The Greyhound. The Lamb. The Dog and Ball. The Bell. The Anchor. The Tavern. I turned to see, but it was gone.

The bus glided on, roaring past a post office, shoe shop, sweet shop, flower shop, barber's shop, chemist, off-licence, garage, laundrette, dry cleaners, and hair salon.

The scene flickered and changed every second. Grocery store. Bakery. Billboard. Café. Park bench. Bus stop. Wasteland. Mud puddles. Abandoned pushchair.

In a playground, I spotted swings not swinging, and a rusty roundabout, begging for tiny hands to wake it with a push.

From the top of my bus, I could also see into houses, into

front rooms, kitchens, bathrooms and bedrooms. I could see through flimsy white lace curtains.

I could see pictures on the walls. Dark, ugly furniture. The colour of carpets. Vivid floral wallpaper. Pot ducks on walls. Clocks on the mantelpieces.

My eyes took a snapshot. My brain made a quick judgment. I relished whatever came into view. I latched on to every image, held it for a second and squeezed every molecule of information from it.

White stucco houses. Tiny front gardens. Low brick walls. Painted doors. Terraced houses. Gnomes in a garden. Tudor trim. Weathervane. Leaded windows.

I spotted a red-faced grocer picking apples from a bin. A monk-headed newsagent pulling down jars of sweets from shelves. A man smoking a cigarette and throwing the packet to the ground. Fish and chips being wrapped in newspaper. Meat pies being plopped into white bowls and smothered with gravy.

In a cobbler's shop with shelves bulging with boots and bags, a hunched figure in a leather apron tapped a shoe with a hammer. In a cafe, two old ladies sat together sipping tea from china cups.

I never tired of the shapes and colours that flashed before my eyes. I was transfixed as I watched people coming and going, stopping to chat and greeting one another with a kiss or a hug.

A man, anxiously tapping his pockets for something he had lost, made me smile. I saw the relief on his face when he found what he thought he had lost.

I strained to hear what a man in a hat was saying as he called to a friend across the street. He pointed at his shoes and laughed, but I had no clue what he was saying.

A woman in a raincoat and headscarf sat glumly on a bench and looked as if she was about to cry. Sad? Tired? Lonely? Lost? I watched her to see if someone would go to her. No one did.

From Nottingham, the road was known as Chesterton Road. From the Chesterton end, it was called Nottingham Road.

From the top of the bus, I could see over hawthorn hedgerows into farmer's fields, where there always seemed to be at least one large tree, an oak, an ash, a chestnut or an elm, in a corner.

Before we reached the village of Trowell, I spotted a small wood, nothing more than a sparse cluster of trees, with gaps between the trunks wide enough to permit a walker to wander with ease.

I imagined a carpet of bluebells in spring, a sea of blue flowers, risen long before leaves returned to the trees.

My mind came back to where I was going and why I was going there. I had been invited for an interview for the job of trainee reporter with the Chesterton Messenger and Irremor Valley Journal, a weekly newspaper with a modest circulation of 16,000.

None of this was my idea. I had never been conscious of wanting any job. The mother of a girl I knew spotted an advertisement in the paper and pointed it out to me.

"You could be a reporter. You'd be good at it," she said. Flattered, I sat down and wrote my letter of application.

A week later, I received a reply, asking me to come to the Messenger office for an interview at precisely 6 p.m. on October 17.

Years later, I realised how important that bus ride was and how it was the start of an adventure that would one day take me around the world.

* * *

CHAPTER TWO
CHESTERTON

The bus grumbled and groaned its way up the final slope and came to a collapsing halt in a large, open, hilltop square in the centre of Chesterton.

The bus conductor pulled the cap from his head, tossed his ticket machine under the stairs and dropped his leather money bag onto the seat beside him.

"Market Place!" he shouted. "Everyone off!"

I sprang to my feet. Other passengers did the same, and we all shuffled off the bus in an orderly single file.

The conductor helped an elderly woman off the platform. She thanked him for his kindness. He smiled but said nothing.

I looked around, turning to take in all the sights around me.

In front of me was the town hall, a solid, serious Victorian edifice with handsome brick facade and a sturdy stone, Italianate balcony, and a row of slender, arched windows.

Opposite was the Co-op, a three-storey department store with large glass windows at street level, showcasing everything from armchairs, carpets, and beds to furniture, toasters, and saucepans.

The Co-op was the store of the people. Prices were affordable, variety was abundant, and quality was questionable.

I spotted two pubs, Sir John Warren and the King's Head. They were merely yards apart, less than a minute's walk from one to the other.

The Roxy cinema, with the canopy above its box office decorated with rows of golden lights, sat loud and proud in a corner. The cinema's name, spelt out in four-foot-high letters, hummed in a blaze of pink neon light.

Behind me, St. John's church stood, dark and sombre and forbidding, with black, smoke-stained brickwork and a dominant clock tower.

The cemetery, at the side, sprawled over uneven ground and was filled with a spooky, jumble of broken and wonky gravestones.

Across the square, the town's library was right next to the post office with a small, bright cafe in between.

The cafe owner, wearing a hat and raincoat, was locking up for the night. He switched off the lights, pulled the door shut, rattled it a couple of times to make sure it was locked, and disappeared into the dark street at the side.

My hometown, Nottingham, had a population of over 250,000. Chesterton, called "Chez" by locals, was much smaller, a compact, working-class, hill town with fewer than 30,000 inhabitants.

I had heard of Chesterton. I may have even been there as a child. But I had no memory of having been there. It was all new territory to me.

I had heard about the town's annual fair, held every year on the third weekend of October.

I looked around the market square and imagined it being magically transformed into a noisy, fun-filled fairground, full of whirling rides, flashing lights and shrieks of delight.

I imagined the Big Wheel turning at speed. I could hear the bumping and banging of Dodge 'em Cars, cries from the Ghost Train, the whirl of the Waltzer.

I imagined the air drenched with the sweet smell of candy

floss and toffee apples, the delicious aroma of fried onions on a grill.

I imagined all these sweet and sickly scents combining with the pungent, oily fumes from a line of loud, overheated diesel generators.

Against the perimeter wall of St. John's, I imagined a row of stalls, all huddled together, with excited pedlars handing out tubs of hot mushy peas, sticks of candy floss, and brown bags of brandy snaps and sugary doughnuts.

The square was the heart of the town, the central meeting place, the hub of the community, the place where all the important events took place — the weekly market, the October fair, Remembrance Day ceremony, the lighting of the Christmas tree, and all manner of presentations, ceremonies, and proclamations.

My appointment at The Messenger was for 6 o'clock at the newspaper's office, which I had wrongly assumed was close to the town centre.

I asked a man in a flat cap and baggy trousers for directions. He pointed to Bath Street, a narrow, bending street of shops that swept down a steep hillside like the drop on a roller-coaster.

"When you see the Rutland Hotel, you'll know you're there," said the man. "But it's a good way, mind you. At least a mile, maybe more." He smiled when he saw the alarmed look on my face.

The clock on the tower of St. John's said ten to six. Too late for me to wait for a bus. I decided to run for it.

I had always been a fast runner. I was a natural sprinter and had won many races. It was how I had managed to stay alive by running away from bullies. I had also taken part in cross-country.

At one point, I even ran for the county, so I knew I could go the distance. I just wasn't sure if I could make it on time.

I was dressed for a job interview, not for a cross-country run. I was wearing my best clothes: a dark blue suit, white shirt, neatly knotted blue tie, and black dress shoes, polished as shiny as I could make them.

I had no choice but to run. Desperate, I raced down the hill, dodging shoppers as I bounded along.

The slope gave me momentum. I took long, loping strides. I could feel the hill forcing me to go faster and faster. Each stride swallowed up yards of ground.

I flew past a bank, a pub, a shoe shop, a dress shop, a dry cleaners, a real estate agent.

A shopkeeper stepped out, saw me coming, and jumped back inside, narrowly avoiding a head-on collision. I turned, half looking backwards, and shouted, "Sorry! Thank you! Sorry!"

Instinctively, I knew what each shop was just by glancing at what was in the window, or words on signs: butcher, baker, solicitor, betting shop, cobblers, hardware store.

Everything flashed by in a blur. I ran on in a blind panic without any pretence of composure. I was desperate to be punctual.

In my head, I heard the voice of my old English teacher berating me for arriving late for class.

"Punctuality is the courtesy of kings, Malcolm. Don't you forget it."

"Yes, sir."

Down, down, down Bath Street, I ran. The slope helped me keep a steady pace. It must have been a frightful sight. I noticed people stopping to stare.

Did they think I was being chased? I saw them looking back up the hill to see who was chasing me. A policeman? An angry shopkeeper? A villain with a grudge?

"No, no, I'm late for a job interview," I cried.

I had to reach the Rutland Hotel. I willed it to appear. I wanted to see the sign because I knew then I would be there.

The slope evened out. I zoomed past Boots the chemist, the New Inn pub, a Methodist church, a cake shop, and a jewellery shop. I crossed Chapel Street, Wilmot Street, and Station Road.

I ran off the pavement and onto the road to pass a queue at a bus stop and had to serve around people jostling to get on the bus.

Bath Street slowly levelled out. I realised I was falling as much as running. I felt the strain in my leg muscles. I started to get breathless. My eyes were watering.

Across the street, I saw the Rutland Hotel with warm light radiating from its windows. From quick glances, I could tell the interior was classy.

Outside the hotel, coal miners were waiting for their bus to take them to work. They weren't standing, but were bent down, hunched in a squat position and appeared to be no more than the size and shape of a sack of rags as they rested on their haunches.

I imagined that was how they looked down the pit, crouching in the dark in some tunnel with a black ceiling inches above them.

With emotionless eyes, they watched me, neither showing encouragement nor contempt. They just stared in silent observation. Their heads turned in unison as they followed my progress.

Was it my extreme effort that captured their attention, or the reckless determination of my running? Their faces stayed in my mind for a long time.

Minutes later, I arrived, exhausted and out of breath. I bent over and tried to catch my breath.

The Messenger office was dark. There was no sign of life inside. I was shocked to find the newspaper was located in an ordinary two-storey house with a shop entrance. I had expected something better, something grander, more imposing.

In the window, rows of black-and-white photographs were neatly pinned to a black background cloth.

The photos were mostly of smiling faces. A bride flanked by her bridesmaids. Soccer players holding up a trophy. The mayor, in his hat and gown, at a charity event.

The faces smiled at me, encouraging me, affirming me, as if to say, 'Well done, you made it!'

One face didn't. It belonged to the villain in an amateur drama production. His face glared at me.

"It's later than you think," he seemed to say. "Watch out! I'm coming for you."

CHAPTER THREE
MESSENGER

As I reached for the doorbell, the door swung open, and I was greeted with the offer of a handshake by a tall, smartly dressed man in a grey suit.

"Hello. I'm Dan Wootton, editor of the Messenger. "Come on in."

I stepped into a darkened office, he closed the door with a firm push behind me, and waved me to follow him.

"Good, you're on time. We like that," he said.

A large, old clock with Roman numerals chimed softly, indicating precisely six o'clock.

Mr. Wootton lifted the top of a wooden counter, allowing us to pass through to a doorway and into a dimly lit corridor.

Black-and-white photos in dark, heavy frames lined the walls. In a corner, I spotted a hat rack, an umbrella stand, and a well-used dog lead, dangling from a hook.

I felt as if I had stepped back in time to the days before electricity, days before cars and telephones, to a time long before I was born.

The narrow corridor reinforced this impression with its musty smell of antique furniture, old carpets, and yellowing piles of newspapers.

There was also another gallery of black-and-white photos, this time mostly of long-dead people, all looking serious and proper in dark clothes at solemn gatherings.

Mr Wootton walked ahead of me in the darkness, opened a door on the right, and let a streams of warm, yellow light flood into the corridor.

I was ushered into what felt more like a living room or a bedroom than an office. A large, linen-covered table was cluttered with books and newspapers, pens and teacups, and scraps of paper with illegible words scribbled on them.

The warm light shone from a solitary table lamp, pushed to the back of the table, and the room was further illuminated by soft flickering light from a flagging coal fire in a black iron hearth.

Two rumpled, wingback armchairs faced one another on either side of the fireplace. The backs of the chairs cast long shadows on the walls.

On one of the chairs, a book lay split and left face down, waiting for its owner to return and resume reading.

The title of the book was "What It's Like to Die," and the words seemed to pulse, looming large, then fading, in the flickering glow of the firelight.

An elderly woman, more round and plump than tall and thin, was seated at the table. She had wiry white hair and was wearing old-fashioned, half-moon glasses. Her face was fleshy and flushed, giving her an air of respectability, authority, and distinction.

Her name was Dolly Marlowe. She was the publisher and sole proprietor of The Messenger, the spinster daughter of the late Rev. William Marlowe, who had founded the paper in 1880.

"Ah, Mr. Malcolm, I am so pleased you are here," she said, her face radiant with kindness and sincerity.

I offered my hand, and she shook it very hard, and placed her other hand on mine to keep it in place.

"But, my, why are you so out of breath? Your face is as red as the coal in my fire," she said.

I explained how I had gotten off the bus at the wrong end of town.

"When I realised I was in the wrong place, I decided there was nothing to do but for me to run for it.

"I ran all the way from the market. Sorry. I'm still a bit out of breath."

I was genuinely embarrassed. For my red face. For panting like a winded horse. For being stupid enough to get off the bus at the wrong end of town.

"Oh, don't be sorry, my boy. That was a brave thing to do. I know I couldn't do it. Run all the way down Bath Street. Could you, Dan?"

She looked directly at Mr Wootton, urging him with open, blinking, expectant eyes to show me support and sympathy.

He relinquished under the pressure of her gaze, sighed, shrugged, and blurted out, "Yes, well, yes, very good running."

His empathy was half-hearted, reluctant and lacked conviction, and he quickly regained his composure, snatch up some papers from the table, and gestured that we should move on.

"Okay, let's get down to the business. You want to join us as a junior reporter."

At this point, I began to speak the words I had prepared and rehearsed, anticipating the question to come.

I gushed about being glad of the chance to be a journalist. I expressed my enthusiasm for the job. I talked about the energy I would bring, about my willingness to work hard, and put in long hours, doing whatever was asked of me. Miss Marlowe smiled, and I felt encouraged.

However, I winced when Wootton asked about my education and my qualifications, and in particular, my exam results. I knew my record was not great.

There was a noise at the door, a scuffling and scratching. The conversation stopped. We all looked up. The door was pushed open, and a large red setter padded in.

It spotted me immediately, came up, licked my hand, nuzzled up against my leg and pushed its rather large head into my lap.

"This is Biddy," said Miss Marlowe, with great affection. "Don't worry, she's friendly. Too friendly, I think. Now, come on, stop that Biddy, leave him alone. He's not here to play with you."

"That's okay," I said. "I like dogs." And I began to pat Biddy's head and stroke her back, while all the time trying to gently ease her head and nose out from my lap as politely as possible.

Miss Marlowe ordered her to a blanket next to the hearth, where the coal fire was slowly sinking and the shifting stack of coals was starting to crumble and collapse.

Biddy waddled obediently, if reluctantly, towards the fireplace and collapsed onto a blanket. She rested her head on her front paws and continued to watch me, blinking and closing her eyes as if about to sleep, then lifting her head quickly whenever she heard new conversation.

The interview didn't last long. I went on about how I liked to write stories, how I had written a short story about a teenage boy who got his girlfriend pregnant, and I mentioned that I had written a film script about a lonely boy named Dappy, who spent his days wandering around cemeteries, reading gravestones.

None of this seemed to impress her. Miss Marlowe listened politely and smiled graciously, and then changed the conversation.

What did I think about the pay? It was not great. Twelve pounds a week. Did I understand there would be a probationary period?

I nodded yes to everything. I had no reason to disagree. I had never had a job before. What did I know.

"We've seen other applicants," she said, adopting a more serious tone and lifting and tapping papers into a neat pile.

"All of them are more qualified than you. One is a university graduate. Another is already working as a reporter at a weekly in Buxton. All very impressive, I must say."

I said nothing. What was there to say.

Mr. Wootton said nothing.

Miss Marlowe fell silent, too.

For a few seconds, the only sound was the snap and crackle of the fire. Biddy let out a great sigh.

"Well, I think we're done here," said Mr. Wootton, getting up from his chair.

I rose to my feet, too, and thanked Miss Marlowe for her time. She remained seated, smiled, nodded in acknowledgement, and twiddled with her glasses.

I followed Mr. Wootton out of the room, walking slowly back down the hallway and into the dark and silent office.

"Thanks for coming. We'll be in touch," he said.

Seconds later, I was outside, back on the lamplit street, with the sound of the office door being shut and bolted firmly behind me.

In the dark, I could see halos of light around the streetlights. The lampposts looked like angels with their heads bowed in prayer.

The pavements were empty, but for a few shadowy figures moving up Bath Street, perhaps miners wending their way home.

I felt happy with the way things had gone. I replayed the interview in my mind, but all I could remember was Miss Marlowe's kind face and grandmotherly smile.

Five days later, a letter in a stiff, white envelope, with The Messenger's name embossed in the top left-hand corner, dropped through my letterbox.

Inside, a letter from Miss Marlowe read as follows:

Dear Mr. Malcolm,

We are looking forward to having you with us next week. If you can cultivate a steady approach to work and study to match your enthusiasm with regard to training for a journalistic career, you should do well.

The next six months will clearly show whether you are likely to make a reliable reporter, with a keen interest in the life of the town.

I certainly appreciate your ability to make an entry on time, red-faced and gasping for breath (having arrived via the 3-mile distance end of Chesterton and then run for it!!) - and yet having retained sufficient aplomb to speak clearly, your determination to succeed in the journalistic world given the chance.

You should go far despite the lack of scholastic achievements.

Anyway, here's your chance! We will do all we can to help you on your way,

Yours sincerely,
M.Marlowe."

I was tickled pink.

CHAPTER FOUR
FIRST DAY

"Hello, you must be the new person."

Plump, rosy-faced and dressed all in pink, Brenda Duncan was the first to greet me when I burst through the shop-style door on my first day at the Messenger. The bell above the door was still ringing as I closed it.

Seated, solid and statuesque, Brenda reigned over the large wooden counter in front of her. She exuded confidence, being clearly in control of everything within arm's reach, all the tools of her trade: stapler, scissors, eraser, pens, elastic bands, ink pad, marker, pencil, and notebook.

In her hand, she held a rubber stamp with a shiny wooden handle. To the right of her were printed forms for placing classified advertisements. Words on the forms were written clearly and precisely, and were evenly placed for clarity.

Brenda was also the boss of the switchboard, which she operated using an old-fashioned black phone.

When I walked in, Brenda smiled broadly, as if greeting an old friend, even though we had never met before. The warmth of her smile made me feel welcome. She was clearly expecting me and seemed to know that I would walk through the door at that precise moment.

Brenda had brown eyes and long, blonde hair the colour of corn. This was pulled back from her face and tied in a bouncy ponytail, exposing her chubby cheeks and high forehead.

I had no idea how she recognised me. In my newly pressed suit, crisply ironed shirt, and highly polished black shoes, I no doubt fit the picture of the new person: a neat, well-scrubbed, hair-combed, desperate-to-please kid fresh out of school.

When she greeted me, Brenda was loud enough for everyone in the office to hear.

Jane Partridge, chief bookkeeper, an elderly, grey-haired woman, sat immediately to the left of Brenda and was perched on a high stool.

Mrs. Partridge was tucked well out of sight behind a partition of frosted glass, but still had a clear line of sight to observe all the comings and goings in reception.

She bobbed her head around the glass screen, smiled warmly and said, "Well, hello, hello, welcome, welcome. We've been expecting you! Isn't this all exciting." And she slipped off her high stool and reached over the counter to shake my hand.

The counter in front of Brenda turned a corner to form an L-shape. From behind this stretch of counter, two figures with their backs to me spun around in their chairs and jumped up to say hello. They were Matthew White and Ron Wilson, the paper's senior reporters.

They had been hammering away at their typewriters, creating quite a racket, oblivious to what was going on around them. They stopped typing when they heard Brenda speak their names, swivelled in their chairs, and came to the counter.

Ron was the paper's chief reporter. He was in his mid-30s, tall, with dark hair, penetrating eyes, and a rugged, swarthy complexion that gave him a permanent five-o'clock shadow.

Matthew White was younger than Ron, but older than me, perhaps a little older than Brenda. He was not only Ron's junior in age but also his subordinate in the office, being the junior reporter.

I immediately noticed Matthew had a slight twitch in his left eye, and a tendency to hop and shift from one foot to the other, nervously bobbing as if somehow trying to avoid being studied too closely.

Matthew's most distinguishing feature was his goatee, which gave him a vaguely bohemian look that was further enhanced by his long, dark hair and dishevelled appearance.

I later came to see that his unkempt look and pseudo-artsy, nonconformist nature were really meant to conceal his natural, irrepressible, spontaneous, mischievous self.

When Matthew spoke, he always did it with a wry smile, as if he never really meant what he was saying and was just testing you, humouring you, joking or playing a game with you.

He and Ron reached across the counter, offering a friendly handshake. I responded in kind.

Brenda got up from her stool, lifted the flap in the countertop to allow me through.

"This way," she said. "You're over here, on this side, away from the roughnecks." And she shot a cheeky smile at Ron and Matthew.

She guided me past her work area, past a coke stove, radiating significant heat, and past the spot where Mrs. Partridge sat behind frosted glass.

In the corner, close to the stove, a hunched, bespectacled, white-haired man in his 60s sat smoking a pipe at a large, cluttered desk.

Wearing a patterned tank-top cardigan, he was totally unperturbed by and seemingly indifferent to all the commotion going on around him.

Although it was not even 9 o'clock in the morning, I noticed he was already munching on a large sandwich - beetroot, I thought, judging from the red-stained bread and the distinctive smell. He took a bite of the sandwich between puffs on his pipe.

"This is Harold, Mr. Watson to you," said Brenda. "He's our advertising manager."

Harold didn't turn around. He merely grunted and made a weak gesture of acknowledgement, lifting the hand with half a sandwich in it into the air.

His phone rang. He grabbed the receiver, dropped his pipe into a black ashtray and began talking, but he still hung on to the sandwich, and looked poised to take another bite the second he was done with his phone call.

A few steps more and we arrived in a cramped space, screened from reception by a thin partition of etched glass.

"Here's your new reporter," Brenda announced.

Wedged into a wooden swivel chair at a desk cluttered with old newspapers, Dan Wootton spun around and jumped to his feet.

His shirt sleeves were rolled up, his collar was unbuttoned, and his tie hung loose, giving the impression that he had been hard at work for hours.

"Ah, yes, today's the day, isn't it," he said, making quick eye contact.

"Thank you, Brenda, I'll take it from here."

Brenda clearly would have liked to linger a little longer, but she had to go, and she frowned with disappointment and rolled her eyes.

Dan waited until she was gone, then pointed me to a swivel chair, not as grand as his, at an adjacent desk.

My desk turned out to be an old dressing table, with two side drawers, each with a fancy diamond-shaped crystal knob.

On the desktop rested an old black Underwood typewriter. I squeezed past Dan and lowered myself into the swivel chair.

"This is where I put the paper together," he began, waving his hand through the air to indicate the scope of his domain, which included a small drafting table.

"And this is the diary," he said, leaping up and snatching a clipboard from a hook. Neatly typed in bold, black capital letters on a sheet of white paper were the days of the week.

"This is where you'll see your assignments for the week, all the events, meetings, and stories we need to cover."

He thrust the clipboard towards me to get a closer look.

Behind each entry, there was a name.

Magistrates Court - Ron.

Town council - Dan.

Awsworth parish council - Matthew.

My eyes ran quickly down the list.

County Court - Matthew.

Housing committee - Ron.

Rotary Club - Dan.

There were four or five entries for each day of the week. The word Saturday jumped out at me. My eyes focused on key words: bazaar, fete, rummage sale. I looked more closely at the Saturday assignments.

Queen Street Baptist Church bazaar - Matthew.

St. John's Church bake sale - Matthew.

Cotmanhay Christ Church fete - Matthew.

Chesterton Town game - Ron.

"You should look at this diary every day to see what you're doing," said Dan. "I do the diary every Friday, so you can see what's coming up."

My eyes were wide. I never realised I would have to work Saturdays.

"There'll be plenty of time for you to get familiar with all this," said Dan, spotting the surprise in my eyes.

Mrs. Partridge poked her head around the corner.

"Dan," she said politely. "Coke, please. The shuttle's empty."

"Oh yes," said Dan. "Now that's going to be one of your other duties."

He shouted over the partition to Matthew, who came straight away.

"Coke, Matthew. Show him what to do."

Matthew waved for me to follow him. He picked up a black

coal scuttle next to the stove and carried it roughly out the front door, banging the frame on the way. I followed him.

He reached through a hole in the side gate, yanked on a piece of string, and the gate swung open.

I followed Matthew down a dark, tunnel-like passageway into a cobblestone yard where there was a black mound of coke.

He angrily cast the scuttle onto the coke pile as if he never intended to pick it up again. The shuttle bounced and landed upside down.

"Coke!" said Matthew with irritation in his voice.

"For the stove," he said, then turned and grinned at me.

"Well, this is your job now. I'm done. I'm sick of doing it, now it's your turn. It's always the job of the junior. Now that's you."

I stood looking at him blankly.

"Well, go on," he urged. "Fill it up. It's your responsibility to keep the stove going.

"When they shout COKE, you have to drop everything. Doesn't matter what you're doing. Doesn't matter how busy you are. You have to get up, get this scuttle, and get coke for the stove."

I start to place individual pieces of coke into the scuttle.

"No, no, not like that," said Matthew impatiently. "Like this." And he snatched the scuttle from me and rammed its open mouth violently into the pile, scooped up enough to half fill the scuttle, then emptied it.

"Here, you try," he said. "Mrs. Partridge will let you know when the stove needs feeding. Just remember, when she shouts, 'Coke' or 'Coke, PLEASE' - (and Matthew rolled his eyes as he imitated her) - you must stop what you're doing and get the scuttle. It's a big deal. They don't like it if you're slow or grumpy. You'll see."

I carried the scuttle back into the office. Matthew returned to his desk. I placed the scuttle beside the stove. It wasn't my job to feed the fire. I just had to get the coke.

Mrs. Partridge touched Harold's shoulder, and he grunted, got up, lifted the scuttle and trickled some of the coke into the stove.

Matthew flipped through the pages of his notebook and began typing, but Dan called his name again.

Matthew sighed, grudgingly rose from his seat, and huffed as he padded around the corner, past Brenda, past Mrs. Partridge and past Mr. Watson to where Dan was sitting.

"Matthew, there's a parcel to go. Better show our new recruit how it's done."

With a shrug and another heavy sigh, Matthew waved for me to again follow him. He came to where Brenda was sealing a large brown envelope with sellotape. She handed the parcel to Matthew with a smirk, knowing how much he disliked what he was being asked to do.

Matthew snatched the parcel from her hands and, without saying anything, nodded for me to follow him out the front door.

I smiled weakly at Brenda and trotted after him.

* * *

CHAPTER FIVE
STAN'S

"What's in the parcel?" I asked.

"Ad copy, stories, photos," Matthew snapped. "The Messenger's not printed here. The printer's in Ripley, 10 miles away. We send copy, photos and ads to them by bus."

His face brightened.

"Another job you'll be doing. And don't get this one wrong or there'll be hell to pay."

We walked side by side down the street.

"You'll also be doing the photo window on Fridays. That's another horrible job I'm stuck with."

I looked confused.

"Every Friday, you take the old photos out of the front window and replace them with new ones.

"It's a pain in the neck, but someone's got to do it. Thank God it won't be me anymore. It takes all morning. And nobody cares. I don't think I ever see people looking at them."

We had only gone a short way down the road when Matthew stopped. He appeared to have thought of something. Whatever it was, it seemed to make him very happy.

"Hey, you feel hungry?" he said. "I didn't have breakfast. Let's stop at Stan's."

We were standing directly outside a dingy cafe with dirty windows streaked with condensation.

"This is Stan's," said Matthew, stepping into the covered doorway. "Now, before we go in, don't be surprised if he insults you. That's just Stan. Just smile and say nothing. Okay? Stan's always angry." And Matthew laughed.

A bell rang as he pushed open the door, but it jammed on the linoleum, and Matthew had to give it a hefty shove.

Inside, a pale, thin, balding man in a stained striped-blue apron emerged from a back room and continued wiping his hands on a tea towel as he came to the counter.

"Oh fuck! What the hell do you want?" he said, tossing the tea towel aside and looking at Matthew.

"The usual, Stanley, my good man," said Matthew in mock civility. "Give me one of your finest fried egg sandwiches. And make it snappy. Now, away with you, my good man."

"Piss off!" said Stan, snatching up a dishrag from the sink and using it to wipe the countertop.

"I'm busy! You come here expecting me to drop everything just to make you a fucking sandwich. Fuck off."

I could see dark rings around Stan's eyes, grey stubble on his chin, and a faint wisp of grey hair on either side of his bald head.

While he was insulting Matthew, he had cracked an egg onto a griddle. He kept talking as he dropped two slices of bread into a toaster.

"Who the fuck's this?" he asked, looking more closely at me.

"He's our new reporter," said Matthew.

"Reporter! Ha! That's a joke. You guys wouldn't know a story if it came up and bit you on the arse."

Matthew said nothing. I could see he neither agreed nor disagreed with Stan. He simply raised his eyebrows and shrugged.

"And what the fuck d'you want?" Stan snarled at me. "Same

as him, I bet."

I looked helplessly at Matthew. I was still shocked by Stan's casual profanity. It came effortlessly from his lips. A lifetime of cursing had made him unaware of the power of the words. Either that or he just didn't care. It was as natural for him to swear as it was to crack an egg or pour a cup of tea.

"He'll have the same as me," said Matthew. "Make it two fried-egg sandwiches. Greasy as you like, Stanley."

"Sod off!" said Stan.

As the eggs crackled on the hot plate, Stan buttered the toast and continued berating Matthew, swearing without inhibition and dropping the f-word every other sentence.

"You fucking walk in here and expected me to wait on you hand and foot," he ranted without looking up. "And for what? For what I ask ... for a fucking egg sandwich. It costs me money every time you come in here. Fucking ridiculous."

The cafe had no tables, no chairs, no stools, no sitting area. It was strictly take-out. Who would possibly come here to eat, I thought. I couldn't imagine how Stan made a living.

As he placed the fried eggs on the toast, he looked up at Matthew, and his tone changed.

"How's that publisher of yours? Miss Marlowe. How's she doing?"

For a second, I could tell that Stan cared and was not just asking about Miss Marlowe to make conversation.

"Oh, she's fine," replied Matthew. "We don't see her much. She comes, she goes, she's in, she's out, always with the dog."

"Biddy?" said Stan.

"Yes, the red setter. She loves that dog," said Matthew.

"I know she does," said Stan. "She's had Biddy for years. I remember when she got her as a puppy."

Matthew looked more keenly at Stan, aware of his sudden show of sensitivity. Stan caught Matthew watching him.

"Dogs, they're a fucking nuisance, if you ask me," said Stan, quickly returning to his old self.

"I see she still has that big car. I see her going out in it and coming back hours later. Always with Biddy. I always wonder where the hell she goes."

"Nowhere," said Matthew. "She just drives around. She goes out to the country, out to the villages and lets Biddy run around. She doesn't have family any more."

I realised that beneath Stan's gruff, off-hand demeanour, behind all the swearing and harsh words, there lurked a residual of kindness — a genuine warmth and gentleness. And for a second, I understood that his fondness for expletives was just his way of being funny or ironic or perhaps a way to hide his true feelings.

Every now and then, his face betrayed him. You could see it in his eyes, in the corner of his mouth, in the way he quickly glanced up at you to see if he had given offence. It gave him away. I could see vulnerability, even generosity. I wondered if he had a wife, or perhaps a son or daughter, someone he loved.

"Do you want sauce with this?" he asked Matthew, speaking in a more friendly, good-humoured tone.

"Yes, please," said Matthew. "Brown sauce, if you have it."

"Fuck you! Of course, I have it. What d'you think this place is - a fucking truck stop. I have brown sauce. I have ketchup. I have it all."

He wrapped the sandwiches in wax paper and dropped them into small white paper bags.

"Here you go. Three and six," said Stan, thrusting the bags towards us.

Matthew handed him two half-crowns and took the sandwiches.

"Now fuck off," said Stan. "And don't come back. I'm busy, I got things to do."

"Thanks, Stan. See you next time," said Matthew.

We stepped out into the cold street with our hot sandwiches steaming in their bags.

As we walked down the street, Matthew tucked the parcel

under his jacket to free up his hands, and we ate our sandwiches with smiles on our faces.

"Good, eh?" said Matthew, showing me his sandwich with the yellow yoke of the egg squeezing out the sides.

"Delicious," I said.

"It's the grease," said Matthew. "It has a bacon flavour from the fat on the grill. It goes perfectly with the fried eggs. Look closely, you can see the tiny bacon bits."

We walked on, enjoying our sandwiches.

"You can always rely on Stan. His bark is worse than his bite," said Matthew. "Nobody knows anything about him. He's a bit of a mystery. I think he was married once, but his wife died. I'm not sure."

"Does he have any kids?" I asked.

"God, I hope not," said Matthew. "Can you imagine them telling you to fuck off."

We laughed.

Within minutes, we were standing at the bus stop outside the Rutland Hotel. In the cold, we stood and finished our sandwiches.

Matthew kept his eye on the corner, looking for the blue double-decker bus to Ripley to appear.

The moment it came into view, Matthew quickly stepped forward to the edge of the pavement so as to be perfectly aligned with where the bus would eventually stop.

The bus arrived, and Matthew handed the bulky, over-stuffed brown envelope to the conductor, who took it without asking questions.

"You have to memorise the number of the bus," said Matthew, pointing at the numbers on the front of the bus, just below the driver's cab.

"Don't forget to write them down or memorise them, if you can. Just don't get them wrong, or there'll be trouble. Just to be safe, I always write down the licence number of the bus, too."

This particular bus was a B2. The number was 687.

"Okay, back to the office and I'll call it in," he said.

"Call it in?" I said.

"Yes, you have to phone the printer in Ripley. Alice always answers. I've never met her, but she sounds like a nice person. She'll recognise your voice after a while. I just tell her the number of the bus, and she goes out to meet it and get the parcel.

"The bus takes about 25 minutes, but you can't wait, you have to phone right away or it doesn't give Alice enough time to meet it and get the parcel."

As we started to walk back to the office, coal miners began arriving to catch the next bus to the colliery.

I watched them with curiosity as they crouched down like African bushmen taking a rest during a hunt. Matthew was still talking about the parcel delivery.

"I know, it's a crazy system, but it works. Some years ago, a reporter went to take a parcel and didn't come back. Nobody could figure out where he'd gone. He was gone for hours.

"It turns out, there had been an accident. The bus's brakes had failed, and it had run smack into some shops on Bath Street. No one got hurt, but the bus was stuck and couldn't move. It was wedged into the shops."

Matthew started to laugh.

"This idiot reporter decided he had to run to Ripley to deliver the parcel. He was gone for hours.

"Dan was furious when he came back. 'What the hell were you thinking?" he said. "What about the accident! Didn't you think that was news worth!' he said."

Matthew paused, then thought of something else.

"Stan thought it was hilarious. 'Call yourselves fucking reporters! A bus crashed and runs into shops and almost kills everyone, and you don't think it's news. What the fuck!"

Matthew did a good impersonation of Stan.

We laughed.

* * *

CHAPTER SIX
TEA TIME

Back in the office, it was tea time. Ten o'clock, the same time every day, was always tea time at the Messenger.

Mrs. Partridge made it, using loose-leaf PG Tips in a big brown Betty teapot. She kept the tin tea caddy, decorated with roses, on her desk for safekeeping, close to the electric kettle.

Each person had their own cup. There were no mugs, only cups with solid handles. Mrs. Partridge was in charge of the tea ceremony.

Work stopped the moment the kettle boiled. Mrs. Partridge tapped one of the cups with a silver teaspoon to announce that the tea was ready to be poured.

Everyone took milk. Mrs. Partridge splashed a drop in each cup before pouring. One spoon was set aside for scooping sugar from a silver sugar bowl. Another spoon was designated for stirring.

It was tantamount to a sin to confuse the role of the spoons. Mrs. Partridge reminded everyone by saying, "Sugar spoon in the sugar bowl, stir-spoon for stirring."

Biscuits were obligatory, usually plain shortbread or ginger.

And the rule was to stand next to the stove, sip tea and make polite conversation.

Feeling she had a closer working relationship with Mr Watson than anyone else in the office, Mrs. Partridge always felt comfortable asking him delicate questions about advertisers.

Did so-and-so like their ad? Would they be placing another? Did they pay on time? Harry usually grunted and gave a terse, one-word response. On this particular day, the conversation was all about me, the new reporter.

"Well, Timothy, tell us about yourself," said Mrs. Partridge.

I blushed, embarrassed to be put on the spot and have everyone's eyes on me.

"Well," I stammered, "The first thing I should tell you is . . . I don't go by the name Timothy. I mean, Timothy is my name, but it's not what everyone calls me."

"What?" barked Dan, a little shocked. "I thought your name was Timothy."

"Yes, yes, it is, that's right, well, that was the name I was given when I was born. That's my Christian name. But I always hated it. And as soon as I could, I changed it. I picked a name I liked, Steve . . . Steven. And that's what I call myself now. It's what all my friends call me, it's what everyone calls me."

"Steve!" said Dan, even more wide-eyed. "But Miss Marlowe and I were calling you Timothy."

"Yes, I know. I'm sorry about that. I'm sorry if you felt deceived. That was never my intention. I didn't say anything at the time. I mean, Timothy is my given name, my official name, the one on my birth certificate. But I changed it to Steve a long time ago, when I was 13 or 14. I don't even remember exactly now how long ago it was, but it was a long time ago. Now, everyone calls me Steve now, even my mother."

The others stood and sipped their tea in silence. They were clearly pondering the ramifications of this revelation, this peculiar deception. Had I meant to deceive? I knew I had not.

I looked at the faces of the people around me and thought I

knew what they were thinking. Is he a trickster? Is he a liar? Is he a con artist? Doesn't this mean he'll get the sack?

Ron broke the silence.

"So, let's get this clear, is your name Ste-FAN with a PH or Ste-VEN with V?" And he smiled as he asked the question, and I could feel the tension in the room dissipate. The seriousness of the moment simply evaporated.

"Hey, this is important," Ron continued. "You know what Dan always says, 'Names sell papers'. We've got to get it right."

There was a gentle mocking tone in Ron's voice, and he smiled at me from behind his teacup as he lifted it to his lips.

"I thought about Stephen with a PH," I said, "but it didn't feel right, so I decided to go with Steve . . . S.T.E.V.E. I still have to sign Timothy on a legal document because that is still my official name."

"Oh dear, this is all too complicated for me," said Dan with a bemused look. He lifted and dropped his eyebrows a couple of times, shook his head, and went to place his empty cup back on the tea tray.

It was at that moment that I felt I knew for sure that I had not been Dan's first choice for the job.

In fact, I knew at that moment the Dan didn't really like me much at all, and this name-change business had only confirmed his worst fears and overall disappointment.

I also knew at that moment that the reason I was standing there was all due to the will of Miss Marlowe. She had wanted it, she had willed it, she had defended me against Dan's criticisms, and, as I was later to discover, she always got her way.

Everyone quickly finished their last sips of tea, followed Dan in placing their used cups on the tray, and returned to their desks, leaving Mrs. Partridge to clean up.

"Okay, enough of this nonsense," said Dan. "Here's your first task."

He dropped a pile of football reports submitted by local amateur teams onto the desk in front of me.

"These come in every week. They're filled in by someone with the team. It could be the manager or one of the parents. We don't allow players to do reports because we don't trust them to be accurate," explained Dan.

He picked one of the reports from the top of the pile and held it up so I could see how it had been completed.

"The name of the team goes here. The home team is always listed first, and the away team, the visitors, is listed second.

"The final score goes here. Below that are the names of all the players who scored, along with the time of each goal. Do you see it?

"Yes," I said.

"Well, pay attention because this is important," he continued.

"Each report gives a simple set of facts, a brief summary of the entire game. Key moments, such as when a player receives a card, is sent off, takes a penalty, or when a substitute enters the game.

"At the bottom of each sheet, here, there are a few more details, such as whether the game was a grudge match between rivals or a cup game.

"Your job is to take all this information and turn it into a simple, straight-forward story.

"Try to imagine you are at the game. Try to make it as interesting and exciting as possible. However, be sure to stick to the facts. Don't go let your imagination run away with you."

The title of the weekly feature in the paper was called Around the Local Grounds. Dan grabbed a copy of the previous week's paper and showed me how it looked.

There were about a dozen match reports, each with its own headline: Tilton Fight Hard For Victory, Disputed Decision Upsets Colts, Hat-trick For Severn, No Drive From Dynamos.

Teams were named after a district, a church, a company, a club, or a workplace. The words were all new to my eyes. There were names and places I had never heard of before. Kirk Hallam.

Granby. Stanton. Marlpool. Cotmanhay. Cossall. West Hallam. Shipley.

Teams' names included Granby United, Kegworth Colts, Ripley St. John, Servowarn, Stanton 1st X1, and Gladstone Y.C. (for youth club).

I had no idea of the colour of the team's strip, the ages of players, and I had absolutely no clue where games were played. I simply had to imagine it all as I sat at my dressing-table desk in my little corner.

Dan turned back to his own work and left me to get on with it. I cranked a piece of rough white copy paper into the typewriter, picked a report from the top of the pile, and closed my eyes and imagined I was on the sidelines, watching the action of a game in progress.

I saw the goalie dive to make a save. I saw a striker tripped from behind and fall face-first into the mud. I saw the ball cleared by a defender, which was then captured by a forward who went on to score. I saw his teammates run to congratulate him, and supporters jumping up and down on the sidelines. It was all complete fantasy, only existing in my imagination.

I opened my eyes and started typing, hammering out a sentence at a time, pausing between lines to read back in my mind the words I had typed.

"The game between Kegworth Colts and Stanton United was a challenge for both teams. Heavy rain had turned the pitch into a virtual quagmire.

"Stanton was doing well, holding its own, but when the ref disallowed a goal, the team was knocked off balance. Kegworth wasted no time taking advantage of Stanton's loss of enthusiasm."

How did I know all this?

Well, I didn't, of course, but I could see from the submitted report that a goal had been disallowed, and a few moments later, the Kegworth team scored, so I felt confident saying "Stanton were knocked off balance" and Kegworth took advantage. It was all fiction.

"Beautiful," I thought, as I scanned my typed words on the paper. It was far from beautiful, but I was having fun.

I loved seeing words appear and pop out of nowhere. It was like magic. Images came to life and jumped straight back at me.

"Shortly after the break, the ref awarded a penalty. Celanese, the centre forward, made sure to extend their lead to 3-nil.

"Despite miserable conditions, Mavers and Straw found the net to bring the half-time score to five-nil."

It all sounded very believable, precisely what happened, just as if I had been right there in the middle of the action.

Throughout my time at the Messenger, I never once met any of the players I wrote about.

For the longest time, I had only the vaguest idea which part of town they played. Week after week, I cranked out dozens of these little stories, each one only five or six paragraphs long.

I always wondered what the players thought when they read them. No one ever called to complain. The stories went out each week and disappeared into homes all over the town.

I liked to imagine the paper being opened on the kitchen table and read by people eating their breakfast and drinking their tea.

I was never given a byline, so my identity was never revealed - a good thing, I thought, especially when I once got a little overconfident and wrote more daring lines - daring for me.

"Gladstone showed no mercy to league leaders Bemrose Athletic" and "after the break, a demoralised Ripley limped back on to the pitch."

Were they really "demoralised"?

Did they really "limp"?

All a question of perspective, I told myself.

The way I reasoned it, how could a team that was losing 6-1 not feel demoralised?

And if the pitch had become "a mud pit from torrential rain" (as the eyewitness reported) and the star player had been brought down in a vicious tackle from behind and afterwards "limped away", well, was it not perfectly reasonable to assume the team, as a whole, had been weakened and "limped" in the second half, disheartened and demoralised. I thought so.

When the football reports were done, Dan handed me the weekly batch of wedding reports.

Like the football reports, these were also dropped through the letterbox every Monday morning.

The wedding reports also gave me the basic facts. Name of the couple, bride and groom, bride's maiden name, usually recorded as "nee" this-or that.

The wedding sheet told me everything. Where the ceremony took place. Number of guests. Names of bridesmaids. Name of best man. Names of parents. Names of other key attendants. Ring-bearer. Flower girl. Matron of honour. And so on.

The forms detailed the style of the wedding dress, the type of bodice used, as well as who made the bouquets, who supplied the church flowers, and where the reception was held. They also included information on the number of people attending, where the couple went for their honeymoon, and the location of the wedding.

These details were filled in by the couple in advance, but completed sheets were not pushed through the office letterbox until Monday morning after the wedding, usually by the bride's mother or one of the bridesmaids.

'Your job,' said Dan, 'is to preserve the magic of the occasion, but don't get carried away.' Always stick to the facts provided."

Dan got me started by giving me a few simple, formulaic sentences to work with, such as "the bride wore . . . "she was accompanied by bridesmaids . . . the reception was attended by XXX-number of people."

"Try to be creative. Switch things around a bit for variety," said Dan.

"You could say, 'Off on their honeymoon to Spain are Bob

and Janice Smith, who were married Saturday at Christ Church blah blah blah. Then, go into all the other nonsense about bridesmaids and flowers."

Once I was familiar with the format, I could whip through wedding reports in no time at all. It was a straight-forward process, but I enjoyed it and found it relaxing.

I knew all the linking phrases and just had to fill in the gaps. For the first time in my life, I knew what a bodice was. I knew the "empire line" was popular, and I knew bodices could be embroidered, sleeveless, beaded, A-line, strapless, or princess.

"It's okay if you can get the name of the church wrong," said Dan. "You can misspell the best man's name, but you can't get details of the bride's dress wrong, or, God forbid, the names of the bridesmaids and colour of their dress. You'll never hear the end of it."

This was how I spent my first morning at the Messenger, writing football and wedding reports.

The keys on the old Underwood tended to stick, being gummed up wth dirt and dust from lack of use. The ink ribbon was worn, old, thin and dry. Yet the typewriter's keys still hammered out legible letters.

Dan rewrote most of what I did, striking out words in red ink and writing new words above the ones crossed out. He rearranged sentences, moving them and entire paragraphs up or down.

When he handed back my pages, I could hardly see my words for red ink. Each page was a jumble of corrections. I was told to retype everything. And to do it quickly.

It was unlike any pressure I had experienced before. For a poorly educated, secondary modern schoolboy, it was a steep learning curve, but I loved every minute of it.

* * *

CHAPTER SEVEN
THE RUTLAND

When the clock on the office wall chimed 12, Ron popped his head around the corner and told Dan he was taking me to the Rutland for lunch to meet the "others".

"Don't let them lead him astray," Dan said.

The interior of the Rutland Hotel was warm, cosy and a little luxurious, just as I had imagined when I ran past on my way to my interview.

The moment we stepped inside, Ron was warmly greeted by Helen, a small, pump, middle-aged waitress, wearing a smart, tightly fitting navy-blue dress that made no attempt to conceal her curves and bulges.

"Having your usual, Ron?" she asked, without looking up as she made her way carrying dirty dishes to the kitchen.

"Round of ham and cheese and half a bitter, thanks, Helen," said Ron.

Helen paused before disappearing into the kitchen and called back down the corridor to us.

"Same for you?" she said, pausing to look directly at me.

I nodded and followed Ron into the main bar, which was decorated like a room in a manor house with pictures of fox-hunting on the flamboyant, green Regency wallpaper, and lavishly upholstered armchairs grouped around dark wooden tables.

In a bay window, three men were already sitting together, each with a half-pint of beer and a plate of sandwiches on the table in front of them.

"Steve, this is Barry Bushnell and Peter Thompson, from the Derby Telegraph, and Rory Michaels, from the Nottingham Post."

They took turns rising from their seats to shake my hand and just as quickly settled back down.

"This is our opposition," said Ron. "They look friendly enough, but we tell them nothing. Remember that!"

Everyone laughed.

"Now, now, Ron, let's be fair. We help one another. We've all friends here," said Barry, who was old enough to be everybody's dad and was the most experienced and respected reporter there.

"It's different when we're on deadline," said Ron, speaking directly to me but also glancing at the others.

"These guys usually have to file their story right away since they're working for dailies," Ron continued.

"We have more time, being weekly, but a scoop's a scoop and then it's every man for himself. But, yes, you're right, Barry, we're all friends here and we do help one another, if we can."

Barry Bushnell had been chief reporter in the Telegraph's branch office on Bath Street for longer than anyone could remember.

He was short with a perfectly rounded head, about the size and shape of a small melon. His face showed kindness and intelligence, his eyes were dark and wily, and his small, quick hands were brown, bony and dotted with liver spots. But by far his most distinguishing feature was his perfectly formed, spherical, balloon-like, semi-bald head with old, wrinkly skin drawn tightly over bony cheekbones.

I thought it was difficult to see how such intelligence and

wisdom could fit into such a tiny skull. Another thing I didn't know was that Barry could do Pitman's shorthand at 200 words a minute, something that everyone talked about with great admiration. What was equally amazing was that he could read back his notes as fast as he had written them down.

No one could match Barry's note-taking. At the end of any event, everyone rushed to check their quotes with Barry. He was never happy to oblige, but reluctantly, he did, but not without showing his disdain with a huff of impatience.

Peter Thompson, his colleague at the Telegraph, was a young father in his 30s, taller, with a tendency to stoop, perhaps from constantly having to bend down to catch what Barry was saying as they walked alongside each other in the street.

Peter was more relaxed and less intense than Barry. He was also more flexible and less haughty, with a kinder, more compassionate, and more empathetic way of dealing with people. This worked well for him and helped him get stories.

He had one particularly noticeable trait, a nervous habit of continually brushing his hair back from his forehead. If he didn't do this, he shook his head instead to throw back his hair. This had become so habitual that a casual observer could be forgiven for thinking Peter had a nervous twitch.

Walking down the street, he was easily recognisable because he wore the same clothes every day: a well-worn gaberdine raincoat over a sloppy, ill-fitting dark green suit. It was his trademark look, but it gave him the air of a stereotypical, overworked, world-weary journalist.

If people didn't know he was a reporter, they could be forgiven for thinking he was the history teacher from a secondary modern school, a clerk in the council offices, or perhaps an overworked, underpaid salesman in the furniture store.

In full flight, on deadline, as he raced back to the office, Peter looked like a giant heron with wings flapping wildly in a panic to gain sufficient speed to fly away.

Rory Michaels, a redhead, slightly older than me in his mid-20s, was the most well-educated of the group. Born in Luton, he spoke with a refined upper-crust accent, having been raised in a prosperous middle-class family and having attended boarding school, as well as Oxford University, where he dropped out before completing his degree.

How he ended up in Chesterton was a mystery to everyone. He looked a little sickly, pale and undernourished with a perpetual spotty complexion.

His social awkwardness gave him the disarming, even charming, demeanour of a bumbling but essentially harmless, well-meaning intellectual.

When Ron came to the table, Rory jumped up nervously as if he had done something wrong and needed to apologise or was about to be reminded to do something he had already been asked to do.

His eyes darted anxiously from face to face as he studied everyone to make sure he didn't miss a cue or the need to give a response.

He waited until all the others had shaken my hand before doing the same, and he did it three times, fearing he had done it wrong the first time.

Ron's order of sandwiches and two half beers arrived. Helen placed them on the table, pushed them closer to us and left without saying a word.

It was all part of the routine. The round of sandwiches consisted of one whole sandwich sliced into four equal triangles, stacked on edge in a neat row. The beer came in classic, dimpled half-pint mugs.

Ron pointed me to my plate of sandwiches and urged me to drink my beer. When I lifted the mug, everyone reached for theirs, and Barry Bushnell initiated a chorus of cheers.

"So, Steven, did Molly or Dan hire you?" asked Barry.

"Both, I think. Well, they both interviewed me at the same time," I said.

"Miss Marlowe hired him," Ron interjected, making sure Barry got his facts right.

"Ah, you're one of Molly's boys," said Peter. This made the others titter.

Ron looked at them dismissively and sipped his beer.

What Barry meant by "one of Dolly's boys" was unclear. I wondered if Ron and Matthew were also "Molly's boys". Were we all impoverished souls who needed someone kind to intervene and save us?

I sipped my beer and pondered. Eventually, I came to believe Barry did indeed believe Molly Marlowe, in her strange, curious, Christian way, wanted to help people who might otherwise get overlooked or ignored.

I was comfortable with all of that. For whatever reason, Miss Marlowe had taken pity on me and decided to take me on as a project.

The conversation at the table shifted to more pressing issues. Stories of the past weeks. The mayor's faux pas at a committee meeting. News of a fact-finding task force at the ironworks.

However, Rutland lunchtime conversations always came back to the same core topics: hirings, firings, circulation figures, union business, bullying editors, and drunken reporters who had made a complete arses of themselves.

Peter always asked what everyone was being paid for their "tea allowance", the expense money allowed for an evening meal before a night assignment. Peter was obsessed with this issue and was never happy with his "tea allowance." He always said he could never get a decent meal for 10 shillings.

"It's ridiculous! How do they expect us to survive on that pittance?" he ranted.

Barry Bushnell always asked about Harold Watson and his garden. Ron always gave him an update.

"Harold's still growing vegetables, still bringing beetroot sandwiches to work, still boasting about the size and juiciness of his tomatoes," he would say.

Lunchtime at the Rutland was a congenial affair. Civil. Chatty. Polite. Friendly. Everyone knew the rules and learned to steer clear of sensitive subjects, such as why the Post had only one reporter in town while the Telegraph deemed it necessary to have two.

Rory apparently found himself in hot water at one lunch when he made fun of the Telegraph for needing two reporters to do the job he was doing single-handedly. After that outburst, lunch gatherings were suspended for a whole month.

We sipped our beers, ate our sandwiches, and settled our bill with Helen. Barry gave the signal that it was time to go when he got up from his chair and put on his coat. We did the same, slowly following him out the door, where there were handshakes and polite farewells before we nodded kindly at one another and went our separate ways.

That was lunch at Rutland.

On our walk back to the office, Ron gave me some advice.

"Be careful of Rory. He'll ask what you're up to and then use it if he can. Barry and Peter know the rules. They'll help you if they can. But don't expect much from Barry. Peter's your man every time. He's the best of the bunch."

The moment we stepped into the office, Ron got back to work at his typewriter, moving quickly from notebook to keyboard. I went back to my dressing table and got on with more wedding reports.

At 5:30, it was quitting time. The light outside was already starting to fade. Street lights were coming.

"Well, that's it for today," Dan announced, rolling down his shirt sleeves and pulling the cover over his typewriter.

"Where do you live?" he asked me.

"With my mother in Nottingham," I said.

"Oh, that will never do. You can't go back and forth like that every day. You'll need to find yourself a place here in town," he said and he called over to Brenda.

"What rentals do we have in classified? Steven needs a flat or something, here in town."

Brenda went away and returned with galley proofs of the upcoming For Rent ads.

"This'll give you a head start," she said. "Nobody sees these till the paper's out on Friday, so you'll have your pick."

I took the proofs, folded them and stuffed them into my jacket pocket.

"Look those over tonight," said Dan. "You can take time off and go see some places tomorrow. Maybe you'll find something before the weekend."

With that, he moved towards the door where Mrs. Partridge, Mr. Watson, Brenda and Ron were waiting. Matthew had left early to cover a council meeting.

"Night," said Dan.

"Night," we all said in unison and stepped outside. Dan flicked a switch, and the office was plunged into darkness. He pulled the door shut with a thud, and it locked automatically.

In a second, everyone was gone. Dan crossed the street. Brenda got into a waiting car with its engine running. Mrs Partridge and Mr Watson walked together towards Bath Street.

I stood and watched as they all vanished into the darkness, then turned and looked back at the black-and-white photographs pinned in the window. I adjusted the collar on my overcoat, turning it up against the chill of the autumn air. A gust of wind pushed leaves into the doorways of shops as I went to get my bus.

* * *

CHAPTER EIGHT
OUTING

The office was already abuzz with activity when I arrived the next morning. How could it be so busy and bustling with everyone working so hard, so early, and so quickly, I thought.

The office had only just opened at 8:30. Yet Brenda and Mrs. Partridge were already on the phone, asking for payments, receipts and explaining advertising rates.

Ron and Matthew were rattling away at their typewriters. Matthew rocked side to side in his seat as he typed like a pianist at the keyboard of a grand piano.

Ron flipped through the pages of his notebook, scrutinising notes scribbled and scratched in ballpoint.

For a moment, he was frozen in thought, then, having found what he was looking for, he went back to rat-a-tat-tatting on the typewriter.

He had no idea how to type correctly. He had trained his fingers to find each letter on the keyboard, and his nimble fingers flashed rapidly, effortlessly, without hesitation over the keys, causing slender metal shafts to catapult black letters from the dark alphabet onto the thin, worn ink ribbon.

The bustle of the office was mesmerising and a little intimidating. The clatter of typewriters. The ringing of phones. The opening and shutting of drawers.

The pungent aroma of coke burning in the stove. The sound of papers being shuffled and stacked. The thump of receipts being stamped and stamped again.

This intoxicating cacophony struck me both as startling and thrilling. It made the office feel gloriously alive and exciting.

The atmosphere made me feel as if I had just arrived at a party. I fell in love with it immediately.

From that day forward, I never stopped loving the sound of a newspaper office at its busiest, at full-tilt as it rattled and raced to catch a deadline.

I never grew tired of the optimism I felt when I stepped through the door and arrived at work each morning.

Nevertheless, I was astonished this day to see such industriousness, drive, and energy so early in the morning.

I glanced at the clock on the wall and felt the need to catch up. I wasted no time getting my coat off and settle down at my little dressing table.

Dan Wootton came around the corner. The sleeves of his shirt were already rolled up, and his tie was loosened. I got the impression he had been working hard for hours.

"Miss Marlowe is waiting for you outside," he said. "She wants to take you around."

I looked puzzled. Should I go or should I wait? I was confused.

"Well, go! Get on with it. Get your coat. Go!" Wootton yelled impatiently, waving me away to the door.

Outside, I found Miss Marlowe stooping to get a closer look at the photographs in the window.

She was elegantly dressed in a dark green tweed jacket and skirt, a plain burgundy cloche hat and shiny black shoes.

She looked like an Edwardian aristocrat in a Country Life

centre-spread, and she reminded me of the prime-and-proper headmistress from my days in junior school.

"Ah, there you are," said Miss Marlowe as I closed the door firmly behind me.

"Good. Now we can go," she said. "I want to show you something, something important, before you get too far into things. It will be helpful."

Parked outside the office was a big, posh black car, a Rover, the kind I had only seen politicians or royalty riding in on television.

My eyes widened when Miss Marlowe walked assertively around the car, opened the door, and slid confidently into the driver's seat.

Miss Marlowe must have been in her 70s, possibly her 80s. No one knew for sure. I certainly wasn't used to seeing people her age still driving. Everything felt wrong about it.

It was not just her age, but also the size and style of the car that bothered me. It looked far too big for her. My jaw dropped open in disbelief.

Miss Marlowe looked at me, puzzled by my lack of movement. She leaned over so she could see me through the passenger-side window.

"Well, come on! Get in!" she yelled. "Let's get going. We don't have all day."

Miss Marlowe was as round as she was tall. At my interview, she was seated at the table. Now, I could see that she was barely five feet tall, quite a bit shorter than me.

I opened the heavy passenger door and slipped into the comfy leather seat, and immediately became aware that both of us were completely dwarfed by the car's vast and opulent interior with its massive steering wheel, fancy dashboard with all its knobs and dials, and huge glove compartment.

I could barely see over the dashboard. Miss Marlowe was forced to tilt her head back, stretch her neck, and lift her chin to see anything. She looked as if she were standing on tiptoe to peek over a wall into a neighbour's garden. It did not inspired confidence.

I said nothing. I didn't want to make a fuss, but I wasn't comfortable with what was happening.

Once settled in his seat, Miss Marlowe switched her glasses, pulling a pair of plain, circular, silver-rimmed ones from the glove compartment.

She fumbled around in her pocket to find her car keys. After a few tries, she found them, inserted the right key into the ignition, cranked it firmly, and the car immediately roared to a start.

Her foot was already pressing down on the accelerator, and it made the engine scream, which was also extremely alarming.

Twisting sideways, she peered awkwardly over her shoulder, glancing quickly left and right to check for passing cars, then pressed down hard on the accelerator and, in a flash, we shot away from the curb. The sudden jolt of speed slammed us both back in our seats.

Miss Marlowe was no Sunday driver. She showed no abundance of caution, no nervous hesitation, no timid apprehension, and she never looked twice.

She was not asking for permission. She made her decision and acted on it with total confidence.

She gripped the steering wheel firmly and decisively, and her unwavering commitment translated instantly into power, propulsion and velocity. If the car had a voice, it would have said: "We're going fast, fast, FAST!"

We reached the speed limit in seconds, sweeping past parked cars, through traffic lights, over zebra crossings and across junctions with a confidence and nonchalance that felt like giddy, reckless abandon.

Miss Marlowe looked like a schoolgirl at the wheel, laughing and giggling as she careened along on a crazy joy ride.

As we zoomed into town, I noticed people stopping to stare. Eyebrows were raised. Mouths were open. All they could see was a big, black, expensive car racing along with no one at the wheel.

All they could see was a small hat bobbing above the dashboard, the only visible part of Miss Marlowe poking up from the driver's seat.

I imagined they also caught a glimpse of a ghostly, anxious, wide-eyed, traumatised young man, sitting bolt upright and rigid, staring out the passenger window with fear and trepidation in his eyes.

We rocketed up Bath Street. "We must surely be breaking the speed limit," I thought. "This has got to be illegal," I told myself. "Laws are surely being broken."

Miss Marlowe repeated her reason for the outing.

"You need to know the town, the different areas and neighbourhoods, the community," she said, speaking as calmly as if she were pouring us each a cup of tea in her kitchen.

"You need to know them all, all the neighbourhoods: Cotmanhay, Kirk Hallam, West Hallam, Little Hallam, Cossall, Stanley, Shipley, Morley, and the rest."

She looked at me to see if I was paying attention.

"Do you understand what I'm saying?" she snapped.

"Yes, yes, I do," I replied, nodding to reinforce my answer. I kept nodding, not wishing to give offence.

"The Messenger covers it all. We go to all the parish meetings. You'll be doing that. You'll attend all the council meetings. They're boring, but necessary."

She looked over at me again to make sure I was listening.

"People know what is going on in their own village, but they want to read about it in the paper.

It confirms what they already know, and they appreciate seeing it written down in black and white. It makes them feel part of the community, I think.

"Anyway, you'll be going to all the villages. To Awesworth, Trowell, Shipley and Stapleton. We even have readers in Kimberley and Eastwood.

"Not as many as we once did because now they have their own paper, but the Messenger still sells in those places. The people there still read us. Do you understand?"

I nodded and kept nodding, but I'm not sure I did understand.

* * *

CHAPTER NINE
TRUTH

At the top of Bath Street, we drove into Market Place, the square in the centre of town. It was deserted but for a short queue waiting for a bus and a few women carrying bags of groceries.

Miss Marlowe swung the car in a dramatic, sweeping semi-circle and came to an abrupt stop opposite the church.

"You know this place, I think," she said as she turned off the engine.

"This is where you got off the bus at the wrong end of town and had to run for it."

She looked at me and chuckled.

Inside the car, all was silent but for the sound of a passing motorcycle and the muffled voices of people talking at a bus stop.

A sudden gust of wind rocked the car, but all outside noise was muffled and muted by the car's windows and plush interior.

"It's quite a way from here to the Messenger. You must have run fast?" she said.

I said nothing. I could see she was enjoying holding the

image of my sprinting down Bath Street in her mind. It still amused her.

I got to hear her tell the story a few more times, as she always insisted on telling it whenever she was with a friend or business acquaintance, and I happened to be in the vicinity.

It became one of her favourite anecdotes. She would start the same way. "Let me tell you about this young man here …" And off she would go. She always finished it with the exact same phrase, the one she had used in her letter of appointment to me: "Thought exhausted and breathless, he still had sufficient aplomb to convey his eagerness to succeed in journalism. What do you think of that?"

The person listening to the story always smiled politely and said something gracious and affirming, as if patting a dog or encouraging a child to keep practising their times tables. "Oh, jolly good!" or "Good for you" or "Well done, you."

Sitting side by side in the car, we stared out the front window. Miss Marlowe pointed at the church behind the low stone wall in front of us.

"That's St. John's. You'll go in there one day soon. It's historic. Dates back to the 14th century. I think it's beautiful, don't you? Not everyone agrees, of course. It had a spire once upon a time, but it was destroyed when it was struck by lightning."

She swivelled in her seat to look over me and out of the window on my side.

"Over there is the library. Do you see it?" She looked at me for a sign of acknowledgement. I nodded.

"It's Edwardian, built with money given by Andrew Carnegie in the 1920s. Seven thousand pounds or something like that. Well, money from the Carnegie charity, anyway. Pretty building, isn't it? I like it."

At this point, she cranked the handle beside her and pushed the door open.

"Let's get out," she said. "We can't see everything from in there."

We clambered out, slamming the hefty doors behind us, and I moved to stand next to her. The sudden chill of the air made me shiver after the warmth of the car, and I buttoned up my jacket.

"Over here is the town hall," said MissMarlowe, waving her hand as if she were painting a picture or somehow magically conjuring up the building out of thin air.

"Do you like the balcony?" she asked. "Someone had Verona in mind when they added that. I'm not sure I like it. Too Italian for my taste. Well, maybe it just tries too hard to look Italian."

She paused and stared more intently at the town hall, and it occurred to me that she was weighing the harshness of her criticism, mulling over whether she was fair or not. She tilted her head, pulled a face as if in doubt, and I took this to mean she thought she might be right or she might be wrong.

"The town hall is where our courts are held. County court. Magistrates court. The magistrates' court is every Thursday. You'll be going there a lot.

"Most cases are small potatoes. Shoplifting. Petty theft. Minor assaults. Breaking and entering. Lots of drunkenness and loutish behaviour.

"Chesterton has a lot of bad drivers, it seems. Driving offences account for the majority of the court's time. Due care and attention. Driving without insurance. Driving without a licence. Driving without an M.O.T., Stuff like that. All very minor. All of it could be avoided if people simply paid attention or obeyed the basic rules. It's not rocket science. The Messenger reports it all. Every case. Every name. Every address. All the fines. Our readers are interested in knowing who has been fined and for what.

"Sometimes you get a special case, something a little more unusual. Perhaps a robbery, arson, or murder. But all the serious cases get sent on to the higher court, the assizes, in Nottingham or Derby."

I listened dutifully, nodding occasionally to indicate that I was listening. But it was all new to me. I wasn't even sure what she was talking about most of the time.

I didn't think I was allowed to ask questions, but later on I realised I was wrong. I could have asked all the questions I wanted to ask because Miss Marlowe loved nothing better than being asked questions she knew the answer to.

"Over there, a little ways down Wellington Crescent, you'll find the main police station."

She pointed to the Co-op store on the corner, then moved her hand to the right to guide my eyes over to the police station.

"It's the pretty little building over there. Red brick. Do you see the nice entrance, the lovely old windows? We send a reporter there every morning to find out what's been happening overnight.

"The constable at the desk will tell you everything. He writes it all down in a big book. You'll see it. He'll open the book and read out the list of incidents. It's like a sermon."

She tittered at the thought, then stopped herself as if she realised it was wrong to find it so amusing.

"Most incidents involve yobs getting drunk, or vandals writing on walls, or petty thieves stealing lead from a church roof.

"We have a good relationship with the police. They tell us everything. It works for them, too. They get people calling them with tips and information after reading about it in the paper."

A flock of pigeons landed in the square. They walked around, pecking at the ground, then something alarmed them, and up they went into a great cloud of flapping wings. They circled in a smooth, synchronised glide over the church, over the square, over the town hall, and disappeared into a back street.

The clock on the church tower struck 10 o'clock. Miss Marlowe looked at her watch, opened the car door, and slipped back into the driver's seat. I got in beside her.

The flock of pigeons returned, circled a couple of times, and then landed directly in front of the car. Miss Marlowe frowned and pressed the horn. The blast sent the pigeon back into the air. They circle again before settling on the roof of the police station.

"They probably belong to someone who lives in one of the terraced houses over there," said Miss Marlowe. "I never understand the appeal of keeping pigeons, but it's something people do a lot here."

I expected us to move on, but Miss Marlowe clearly had something to say. I thought it would be about pigeons, but no.

"Do you know what all these places have in common?" she began in earnest. "The church. The police station. The library. The magistrates' court. They all have something in common."

"They're all located here, in the same part of town, around the square?" I ventured, feeling pleased to have thought of such an obvious common denominator.

"No, that's not it," said Miss Marlowe. "What they have in common is that they are all, in their own unique way, try to tell people the truth.

"The library, the church, the courts, the police, they all have the job of telling people something they can believe, something important, something that is real and true.

"Do you see what I am saying? This is precisely what we do, or at least we try to do, as a newspaper. We give people the facts, truths they can make sense of and put to good use.

"It's our job to provide them with accurate information, something they can trust, rely on, and know for sure. Facts and truth are two sides of the same coin. A fact is irrefutable. Same goes for truth. Truth doesn't change. It is what it is: incontrovertible."

She glanced around the square, her eyes moving from the church to the town hall to the police station to the library.

"You see the library over there. It's an important and valued source of information. It's filled with books. And the best books, the ones people like the most, I believe, are the ones that are most accurate, ones filled with information you can trust.

"Even the best fiction stories have at their core a truth, something we know to be real. I think they must have, or we wouldn't read them."

She moved her head to look directly at the police station.

"The police are not perfect, but they are always trying, in their own way, clumsy at times, I know, to get to the truth.

"They want to gather the facts of the case, and find out what really happened. They need to get the facts right, get to the truth, when they arrest someone, or they don't have a case.

"Like us, they have to ask questions and find the right answers to get to the nub of the matter, to uncover the truth."

She turned and pointed at the town hall.

"The courts are held in there. When you go, you'll see a row of magistrates, two or three of them, sitting together. They're called that *the bench*. Magistrates are supposed to be good listeners. They listen to what the police say. They listen to what the solicitors say. They listen to what the accused person has to say.

"Then, they try to discern the truth, to figure out what actually happened. Only then can they decide if someone is guilty or not. It all comes down to finding out the truth.

"You know people swear to 'tell the truth, the whole truth and nothing but the truth." But they often don't. They often lie. Some people struggle to tell the truth. They only know how to lie to get what they want or to get themselves out of trouble.

"The job of the magistrates is to listen for the *ring of truth*, not just what makes sense, but what sounds like reality, what really happened. They have no time for lies and deceit. They just want the facts, the whole truth, and nothing but the truth."

"What about the church?" I said. "Does the church tell the truth?"

Miss Marlowe smiled, then frowned and tightened her lips. Her eyes widened and her eyebrows lifted, and her expression was a mix of disappointment and optimism, like the face of a mother weary of a child's disobedience but committed to still love and cherish.

"Did you know my father was a minister?"

"No," I said.

"Well, he was. And quite a good one. He was also mayor for a few years. I consider myself a Christian, so I think I know quite a bit about the church," she said.

"This church. St John's, believes it is telling people the truth. It believes in right and wrong. It believes it knows how people should behave and what they shouldn't do. So, yes, In its own way, I would say the church is committed to telling the truth.

"It gets a lot right. I think we all agree that it's better to be kind than cruel, better to love rather than hate, and better to tell the truth than tell a lie.

"I believe in turning the other cheek and returning good for bad and going the extra mile and all of that. Do you see what I'm saying. The church is deeply concerned about what is true, what is most important. And telling the truth is also our business, the newspaper business, is what we're all about."

Miss Marlowe laughed a little after saying this and smiled as she started to formulate her next statement.

"I'm old-fashioned. I believe truth is like a stone. It's strong and unbreakable. That's why it is so important. You need to make sure your stories are always honest and truthful and contain all the facts.

"That's what people want. And they can feel it in the writing. If you stick to the facts, you'll have done your job. And that's all I want you to do."

Miss Marlowe stopped talking and began rummaging through her jacket pocket for car keys. She found them, opened her car door, and climbed in. I got in the passenger side. Awkwardly, she fumbled again to find the right key in the ignition. She turned the key, and the car sprang to life and started vibrating.

"Don't forget," she said, looking me straight in the eyes.

"Your job as my reporter is always to tell the truth. That's what all the best reporters do.

"It's not your job to pick and choose the facts. Just tell it like it is and let the reader decide. Understand?"

I nodded, but once again, I wasn't at all sure I did understand.

The car lurched forward, and we were off, speeding away from the square, along South Street, and down the hill in the direction of Nottingham.

CHAPTER TEN
HEMLOCK STONE

We slowed down to cross a bridge over what seemed to me to be little more than a trickle of a stream.

"That's the mighty Irremor," Miss Marlowe said drolly. "It doesn't look like much, does it. That's the same Irremor in the name in our masthead, Chesterton Messenger and Irremor Valley Journal."

Miss Marlow pulled to the side of the road and directed me to look out the window.

"Have a closer look. It's not the Thames, Trent, Ouse, Derwent or Cherwell. You don't get a mighty rush of water with the Irremor. In fact, you don't get a lot of water at all."

It was not an impressive sight. It looked more like a stream than a river.

"I must have crossed it when I came on the bus, but I don't remember seeing it," I said.

"You wouldn't. Look, it's so small, puny really," said Miss Marlowe. "In some places, it is not visible at all. It completely vanishes.

"It comes down from Kirkby-in-Ashfield and twists and turns till it empties into the Trent. You know the Trent, of course?" she asked and gave me a look that suggested she would be disappointed if I said no.

"Yes, of course. It's Nottingham's main river. I've walked beside it many times. I even went canoeing on it when I was at college."

"Well, the Irremor is tiny by comparison," said Miss Marlowe. "But I still like to think it has its place in the world of rivers and that it is known and loved by all the great rivers. Rhine. Nile. Amazon. Danube. Mississippi. I like to think they would give a nod of recognition to the Irremor.

"They say all rivers have a voice. I imagine our Irremor has a small, quiet, and unassuming voice, but one that can still be heard and has something important to say."

Miss Marlowe looked pleased with herself as she ruminated on this idea of rivers greeting one another.

"The word Irremor means 'wanderer' or 'wandering'. It's a lot like you and me. We're all wanderers, in our way, searching for something, looking for meaning. Anyway, the little Irremor is our river. It's part of us here, at any rate."

We moved on, and as we zoomed through the village of Trowell with St. Helen's Church on the corner, Miss Marlowe startled me with a question about my change of name.

"Dan tells me you don't go by Timothy. He says you prefer to be called Steven or Steve. Is that right?"

I nodded.

"Why? Didn't you like Timothy?" she probed.

"I thought it was weak," I said. "People called me Tim and Timmy. I didn't like it. And I didn't like the way people treated me when I told them my name was Timothy."

"It's not a weak name," she said, glancing over at me and shaking her head, but her rebuke didn't feel like an attack, more of a defence of the name itself. I imagined she knew, or had known, some Timothys and didn't consider them weak at all.

"After I changed my name to Steve, everything went better. Everyone treated me better. Friends. Teachers. Girls. Everyone."

"Ah, girls!" said Miss Marlowe, smiling as if she had gotten to the heart of the matter. We drove on in silence, with only the sound of the engine, the tires on the road, and the whoosh of air as we sped past parked cars.

"Do you think I was wrong to change my name?" I said, breaking the silence. "Was it a sign of weakness? I was not trying to hide something or deceive anyone, you know."

"Oh no, not at all. You're certainly not the first to change their name because they disliked it. C.S. Lewis, the writer of those wonderful Narnia stories, didn't like the name his parents gave him. His name was Clive, but he hated it and decided to call himself Jack. And that's what everyone called him. Jack Lewis. I think he was only a child, maybe four or five, when he told everyone, 'Call me Jack!'"

She looked over at me and smiled.

"And you know, a lot of people in the Bible changed their names. Abraham was not always Abraham. He was once Abram. Peter was Simon before he became St. Peter. And Paul was Saul before he was known as St. Paul.

"I don't think it's important at all. A rose by any other name and all that. No, no, I don't think it was a sign of weakness, and I don't think you did anything wrong. And I am sure you never meant to deceive anyone."

"No, I definitely did not," I said quickly, "I just feel better being Steve. I like how it sounds more, too."

I went back to looking out the window as hedgerows flashed by, and I caught a glimpse of houses, driveways, and little corner shops.

I could see Miss Marlowe was gearing up to say something more. She lifted her chin, tilted her head up, and fixed her eyes more attentively on the road ahead.

"What really matters is what's inside. That's what really counts. A cup with tea is a tea cup. Pour the tea out, put coffee in, and it becomes something totally different—a coffee cup.

"The cup is not what matters. It's what's in the cup that

matters. Who cares what name you go by. It's what's inside that counts, who you are inside, what you do, what you say, how you conduct yourself. That's what matters."

In Bramcote, we turned left onto Coventry Lane, where, at the top of Stapleford Hill, I could see the Hemlock Stone, a large, jagged sandstone pillar, black at the top and red at the bottom. We pulled to the side of the road to get a better view of the stone.

"Do you know what that is?" asked Miss Marlowe.

"I've seen it many times before," I said. "My father used to drive past here all the time. He always pointed it out."

"What did he say about it?" she asked.

"He said it was a stone the Devil threw at Jesus. That's why the top is black. That's where the Devil held it. I don't remember the whole story. The Devil threw it, and Jesus stopped it. That's why the bottom is red?"

Miss Marlowe shifted in her seat, getting more comfortable before delivering her next dissertation.

"Yes, there is a story that goes something like that. The rock is called the Hemlock Stone. It has been in that spot for thousands, if not millions of years.

"The story your father told you is the one most people know, but it is a little different. They say the Devil got so angry about the sound of monks praying at Lenton Priory, he picked up this stone and threw it at them, but he missed and it landed here.

"There's also another story about the Devil being angry at the sound of church bells ringing. What do you think?" she asked.

"I don't know. They're all good stories," I shrugged. "I like the sound of church bells, but I guess they could drive you mad if they were ringing all the time."

"Ah, but the truth is something else," said Miss Marlowe. "Science tells us the rock is made of two types of sandstone, one harder than the other, one more porous, more prone to pollution than the other.

"The top part turned black from dirt and grime. The bottom was harder, less exposed and did not absorb dirt. At least, I think that's why the top turned black, while the bottom remained sandstone red.

"Now you see how important it is to get to the truth. The Devil story is fun. It's the one everyone likes to tell, but that's not how the stone got here or why it is the colour it is.

"It might have been part of an ancient quarry, or perhaps it was left behind after an earthquake. I'm not convinced the Devil is responsible or that he got upset with monks praying or with bells ringing."

Miss Marlowe started the car, and we moved on. The Hemlock Stone looked sad and lonely against the sky at the top of the grassy hill.

I still liked my father's story best.

CHAPTER ELEVEN
STAPLETON

From Stapleford Hill, we headed back towards Chesterton, turning down a country lane that took us into the pretty village of Stapleton-by-Dale.

Miss Marlowe parked in the heart of the village, close to a large stone cross, the Stanhope Arms pub and a row of old brick cottages.

"It's seven miles in that direction to Nottingham, seven miles that way to Derby," she said.

We stood for a few minutes in the perfect peace and silence of the village, listening to the sound of a robin singing.

The streets were deserted. There was no sign of life, no movement at all. Wherever the villagers were, they weren't in the streets. We saw no one in the field, no one working in the garden, no one going in or coming out of the shop.

"Beautiful here, isn't it?" said Miss Marlowe. "Such a pretty place. It was once a grand estate, but that was long ago."

We walked together and looked over the low stone walls into the gardens, and peeked into the curtain-less windows of the cottages.

In the centre of the village, we came to a cast-iron water pump, dating back to the 1800s, and dedicated to Queen

Victoria. Miss Marlowe put her hand on the pump as if touching an ancient treasure.

It was October, and the smell of smoke was in the air. There were red berries on the cotoneaster and yellow leaves on the ash trees.

All was calm and quiet and serene. We were comfortable in each other's company and happy to be walking together in the sunshine.

"Do you live with your parents?" Miss Marlowe asked.

"I live with my mother," I said. "My parents separated when I was 10. My dad now lives in Beeston with my Aunty Joyce."

"Aunty Joyce?" asked Miss Marlowe.

"I didn't know I even had an Aunty Joyce until I went with my dad to Llandudno for a holiday in the summer. Aunty Joyce was there, staying at the same hotel, the Imperial."

"And your mother? Is she on her own?" asked Miss Marlowe, speaking softly and cautiously.

"It's just the two of us now. It's been that way for a long time. She works at the Players factory."

Miss Marlowe walked a few steps, stopped at the stone cross, and bowed her head, closing her eyes in prayer. I stood beside her, noticing how smart the pattern of her tweed suit looked in the soft autumn light.

We ambled back to the car. Our footsteps were the only sound in the village, but as we slammed the doors, we saw curtains move in the window of one of the cottages, and a small, pale face appeared and disappeared.

From Stapleton, we drove down a narrow, winding lane, lined by thick hedges and rows of trees with dark, bare branches pushed into a blue sky.

Beyond the hedge, I could see open fields. The sun was low in the sky, and a line of white clouds stretched in thin brushstrokes along the horizon.

"It's perfect here, isn't it. Calm, peaceful, tranquil, unspoiled.

We used to call this rustic, bucolic, picturesque, something poetic like that," she said.

She brought the car to a halt at a spot where we could easily see over the hedges and beyond a scattering of trees into open fields stretching and even farther to a distant wood.

A flock of starlings swept up from the ground, circled in a dense cloud and disappeared as quickly as they had appeared, into a neighbouring field.

Miss Marlowe started to quote lines from Shakespeare's Richard II.

"This earth of majesty, this seat of Mars, this other Eden, demi-paradise . . ."

She paused, and I added, "This blessed plot, this earth, this realm, this England."

It took Miss Marlowe by surprise. We laughed.

"Let's see what's down there, shall we?" she said, looking into the lane ahead, although it seemed as if she already knew what we would find. Around a bend, a strikingly different landscape came into view.

"This is Stapleton ironworks," she said. "It's where many of our readers work, where they earn the money to pay their bills."

Instead of trees, hedges and fields, there was a bleak landscape of muddy roads, drainage ditches, gravel patches, work sheds and a network of crisscrossing train tracks.

In the distance, we could see high metal gantries, rows of metal-clad workshops and long conveyor belts running up from the ground.

A dirty forest-green Sentinel train came trundling into view, grinding along as it shunted a string of bucket-shaped hoppers, steaming with hot slag, just drained from a blast furnace.

I could hear the scraping and grinding of the train's wheels, metal on metal, as they rubbed and turned on the rusty tracks. There was also the noise of couplings as they jolted and tightened.

Walking beside the hoppers and alongside the rolling

conveyor belts, I could see groups of dark, shadowy figures. They looked small and vulnerable in comparison to the weight and bulk of the open-topped hoppers.

Men were yelling to one another, waving their arms and shouting instructions. The words were smothered by the clanging of the train as it inched along the track.

"Stapleton makes iron pipes, the best in the world," said Miss Marlowe. "You can see piles of them stacked over there.

During the war, Stapleton made shell casings, bomb casings and air raid shelters. Nowadays, they make spun iron pipes, lampposts and manhole covers.

"One day, you'll get a close look. Stapleton is always inviting us up here to announce something or other. They have award programs and retirement ceremonies. The Messenger covers it all."

We stood scanning the landscape, picking out rolling stock, chimneys, train sheds, tool shops and dark brick buildings with more doors than windows.

"What I want you to remember," said Miss Marlowe, "is that this is where many of our readers work. This is a dirty, dangerous place to work. I don't know how they can do it.

"They say Stapleton makes iron pipes . . . and old men. People work here their entire life. They grow old here. They die here.

"It's no holiday camp. Just look at those work sheds. It's a tough, rough place. The work is hard and physical. It's a scary place. Make a mistake and you can get seriously injured."

"I remember taking a tour here once. Molten metal was flowing like lava. I was scared. It ran in thick, red streams from the furnace into channels carved out on the ground. I'd never seen anything like it."

She went on to paint a grim picture of men with blackened faces, working without masks in tight, enclosed spaces, surrounded by the fumes of gases and molten iron swirling at their feet.

"When you visit, you'll see for yourself, you'll see what I am talking about. Coal piles, black sheds, noisy machines, slag piles and blistering clouds of steam.

"The steam bursts up and shushes at you when you least expect it. It made me jump. It'll make you jump.

"It sounds like hell," I said.

"No, it's not hell. People aren't happy in hell. The men who work here at Stapleton are happy. But, yes, it feels as hot as hell. It's dark and loud with lots of banging and clanging going on. I was mostly scared for the workers. I was sure someone was going to get hurt. But it didn't bother them. They laughed at me."

"Are they well-paid?" I asked.

"Not particularly," Miss Marlowe. "But they don't complain. They tell me, 'We're a community. We're all friends.' They get a gold watch at the end, when they retire. That's all. They deserve much more. "

A group of men walked past the car. One smiled and waved. Miss Marlowe's mood changed. She searched for new words.

"I think the workers here feel lucky . . . lucky they're not down the pit. The colliers have it darker, dirtier, harder. Coal dust's a killer. At least here, workers have some air and sunlight. It's a terrible thing to hear a miner coughing and wheezing."

She turned the key in the ignition. The car rumbled and started, at first making a rasping sound, almost as if imitating the gasping breath of an old-time collier. Miss Marlowe stared at starlings picking at stubble in a field.

"When you see these men, in the pub, in the park, at the football, fishing by the canal, you need to remember that this is where they spend most of their life. Let's never do anything to make their life harder than it already is."

We barely spoke on the ride back to the office. When we arrived, Miss Marlowe waved me to get out. She smiled and waved. It was like a kindly tutor dismissing a student.

* * *

CHAPTER TWELVE
SHEPHERDS

"Any luck with those rentals?" Brenda asked as I walked through the door. Dan Wootton was standing, listening nearby.

"Weren't you seeing some places today?" he asked.

"Yes, I picked out three. I thought I'd go see them this afternoon, if that's okay," I said.

"Yes, go, go!" said Dan, sounding more enthusiastic than I thought he needed to be. "The sooner you're settled, the better. Take the afternoon."

I wasted no time in grabbing my coat and heading out, walking up Bath Street towards the town centre, and as I walked, I wondered where I should stop to grab a sandwich.

I had not gone far when I spotted the familiar face of Rory Michaels, the Post reporter, I had met at the Rutland. He spotted me, waved cheerfully, and crossed the street to say hello.

"Where are you off to?" he asked, pushing hair out of his eyes.

"I'm looking for a place to grab a snack."

"Come with me," said Rory. "I always go to Shepherds. It's on the corner up here. They do really good, cheap dinners."

As we walked together, Rory turned and pointed back down to his office in a bay window upstairs, above a flower shop.

"That's where I hang out. There's only me, so I don't need a lot of room. Just a desk, chair, typewriter and phone. Pretty basic."

Shepherds was already packed with customers when we stepped inside. People were seated six, eight or ten to a table, filling both sides of the room with a narrow space for people to get in and out down the middle.

All the tables had white tablecloths, and the walls were simply painted but left plain and undecorated. Customers were mostly workers from local shops and factories, as well as a few pensioners who had taken the bus into town specially to meet and eat together.

Rory and I squeezed into two seats at an already busy table, close to the back of the room, near the kitchen.

I could see three cooks, in short-sleeved shirts and white aprons, hovering over a row of stoves. Steam rattled the lids of large black pots that tapped and trembled above the hot yellow flames of gas burners.

Two waitresses, one young, one middle-aged, with their sleeves rolled up and wearing floral-patterned pinafores with large pouches, moved quickly and purposefully between tables, delivering meals, placing cutlery, collecting dirty dishes, and wiping up spills and messes.

The waitresses squeezed gingerly behind people eating, taking care not to disturb coats hung casually on the backs of chairs.

People were constantly calling out for things: salt, pepper, more bread, more butter, sugar, a fork, a knife, a spoon, more gravy.

The red-faced waitresses, flustered but not in a panic, answered each demand, saying "in a minute, darling' or "I'll be right there", or "I'm coming", or "I'll be back in a sec, dear."

They never lost their temper or showed the slightest sign of grumpiness. If they saw a simple solution, they used it, reaching between customers to grab the requested salt, pepper, butter dish, fork, knife, spoon, serviette, whatever. They robbed one table to pay another. It worked beautifully.

In this way, they were able to keep everyone happy, and the place hummed and buzzed with cheerfulness, a jolly hubbub of friendly chitchat and lively, good-natured banter.

It was a bustling, chaotic scene with everyone talking at the same time, often with food in their mouth, and perpetually crying out for more - more tea, more milk, more bread.

When it came time to pay, the pensioners, in their impatience, tried to slip on their coats and squeeze out of their seats, moving awkwardly into the gap between tables while all the time feigning not to disturb others and proffering insincere apologies for any unintended, impolite nudge, bump, or jolt.

The weary waitresses pulled leather wallets from the pouches of their aprons, snatched up cash, and just as quickly dispensed change, slapped it down loudly on the table.

Rory caught the eye of one of the waitresses. She recognised him and smiled.

"Yes, luv. What can I get you?" she asked.

"Full dinner, please. And one for him, too."

The waitress said nothing but immediately plonked a plate of sliced bread in front of us and pushed the butter dish towards Rory.

"You get meat and two veg here for four bob and all the bread you can eat plus a cup of tea," said Rory gleefully, and he smiled and nodded to underscore the value and truth of what he was saying.

The waitress returned, carrying two large dinner plates, which she banged down on the table, one in front of each of us. There was no delicacy in the delivery. Plates were delivered and dropped without fuss or explanation.

Each meal contained a generous portion of meat stew, two large boiled potatoes, a heap of cauliflower, a mound of peas, and a rather sad, overdone Yorkshire pudding that looked as if it had just been sat on. Everything was smothered in a thick, dark brown, delicious-smelling gravy.

"Don't worry what it looks like," said Rory, "It tastes fantastic. Trust me. You'll love it."

We tucked in. Rory wasted no time buttering a thick slice of bread. He took a big bite and forked up some meat and cauliflower.

I sliced into my potatoes and scooped up peas. The food was indeed delicious, just as Rory had promised.

"I live alone. This is my only meal of the day. I'm no good at cooking. What about you?" said Rory as the waitress arrived with two cups of hot, steaming tea with the milk already added. She pushed the sugar bowl closer to Rory.

"I still live at home with my mum," I said. "She's on her own, but she'd like me to move out, so I'm looking for a place of my own, a flat or something to rent here in town.

"Found anything?" asked Rory, his mouth full of Yorkshire and potato.

"No, I've got three places to see this afternoon."

Rory was only half listening. He was more interested in devouring the food on his plate.

"If you're smart, you'll come to as many receptions as you can?"

"Receptions?" I said.

"Yes, receptions. We get invited to them all the time. They always put out food, snacks, and drinks."

Rory could see I was confused. I hadn't a clue what he was talking about.

"Receptions. Publicity events. You know, media announcements. They invite us, the Press, all the time, to give us information, stuff they want us to write about. They want it in the paper. But here's the best part: you get to eat and drink for free. You just have to get there early, so you can eat as much as you want before they start talking.

"You don't need to be invited. You just show up. I gate-crash lots of them all the time. They always let me in. You should just come with me. I'll get you in. The Mayor puts on great media events. He likes doing it. He likes the free drinks.

"My favourites are the Licensed Victuallers, the pub people. They have loads of money. No expense is spared. They always put on a good do. Great pub fare. Nice, big sandwiches. Free beer. Everything's free for us. You don't want to miss out. Just come with me."

Rory's red hair was long and unkempt and it made him look like a student or a hippy or an intellectual. When he spoke with his plummy southern accent, everyone thought he was a toff. It always made me smile how they looked at him and how indifferent he was.

All the time he was talking, he was forever nervously looking around as if he feared someone might be listening to his conversation.

As time went by, I stopped noticing this nervous twitch and started to think of his anxiety as simply part of his natural eccentricity. I thought he was kind and harmless, clever and artistic, funny and very knowledgeable.

We ended up liking one another a lot and we spent a great deal of time together, sitting next to each other at council meetings and county court and magistrates' court.

I didn't realise that the day when we went to Shepherds was the start of our friendship. We would be the best of friends for a long time.

After the meal at Shepherds, there was no long, drawn-out goodbye. We paid up, picked up our coats, and left.

"See ya," said Rory. And we went our separate ways.

* * *

CHAPTER THIRTEEN
BISHOP

Xpress, a dry-cleaning shop, a short walk up Bath Street from Shepherds, had a two-bedroom flat for rent, directly above the store, which presented itself as the epitome of convenience. The store sparkled and gleamed and was drenched in bright neon light and looked as scrubbed-clean as a freshly pressed shirt.

The owner, a tall, willowy man wearing a white lab coat with the words Xpress to Impress on the front, greeted me with a firm handshake and rushed to open a side door, leading to a steep flight of steps to the flat.

We tramped up the stairs, he struggled to open a sturdy fire door, and we entered a dark hallway into the living room.

I was immediately drawn to a narrow window balcony overlooking the street, and stood for a minute watching people in the street below without them ever knowing they were being watched.

The sky suddenly darkened, and it started to rain, slowly at first, then turning into a heavy downpour with raindrops hitting hard and bouncing up from the pavement. People scurried to find shelter in shop doorways, or they flipped open umbrellas and went quickly on their way.

In the kitchen, I found a sad, old white sink, stained from age and overuse. On the wall next to it was a clunky white Ascot water heater. A small window, in need of a wash and with a cobweb or two hanging from it, looked directly onto a brick wall.

In the bedroom, I could smell fumes from the dry cleaners downstairs. I felt a sickly tickle in my throat as I breathed in the acrid aroma. I frowned and winced a little.

"You'll get used to it. I did," said the man in the white coat. "It's funny how it goes away." Trust me. You don't notice it after a while. Do you need more time?"

I don't need more time. I knew immediately that I hated it and wanted to get out as quickly as I could.

We hurried down the stairs. I said I would think about it, but I was lying. I knew my mind was already made up.

The man locked the door, flashed me a weak smile, turned and rushed back to the shop where a woman stood, flapping her umbrella to shake off raindrops. The man said it was good that the rain had stopped. I looked up at the sky. Grey clouds were still spitting raindrops on passing cars.

At the top of Bath Street, I turned into East Street, then High Street and finally arrived at St. George's House, a big, old, rambling Georgian mansion behind St. John's.

A high wall separated the house from the grounds of the church, but the clock tower dominated the skyline and loomed over St. George's and its overgrown flower garden.

I rang the doorbell, and Dylan Bishop answered. He was tall with long, scruffy hair, black horn-rimmed glasses, and was wearing an old Afghan coat with embroidered pockets and fur around the collar.

Dylan's face had a rubbery, theatrical look, a kinder version of a Punch and Judy puppet, inoffensive, ugly, but not alarming or unpleasant.

A large, fleshy nose dominated his face, full of bumps, wrinkles and ridges along with thick, rubbery lips that widened, stretched and twisted into a quick, easy grin.

"Good after-gloom," he joked. "No more raindrops falling on our heads. Grey skies are gonna clear up."

I didn't get it, and he tried to help me by pointing at the sky. Dark clouds had mostly disappeared, replaced by patches of blue.

"I'm here to see the flat for rent?" I said.

"Sorry, no flat for rent here. No room at this inn," he said with a twinkle in his eye. "We're full up. And no stables for rent either."

Dylan spoke in a slow, measured way. It made me think he had been smoking dope. He noticed that I was not amused, and he changed his tone and became more serious.

"Are you sure you have the right address?"

He took the paper from my hand and looked at the address on it.

"Well, the address is correct, but I think there's been a mistake. We're all teachers here. Two up, two down. My wife and I live upstairs. And there's definitely no flat for rent. We occupy the whole house."

I heard footsteps on the stairs behind Dylan. A man, a woman and a young girl appeared, then vanished just as quickly into a side room.

I thought they were hippies. The man and woman were young, in their late 20s, and had long hair. They wore faded jeans, brightly patterned shirts, and floppy, slip-on shoes. I was surprised to see them in such a stately, old-fashioned mansion.

From the doorway, I caught a whiff of incense burning, and I could hear someone playing acoustic guitar, accompanied by a flute.

A little way down a dimly lit hallway, I could just see through a partially open door into a room with a wooden floor. The young girl was running and jumping, performing a free-form dance with spinning, ballet-like movements.

It reminded me of a time in my infant school when we were

told to imagine ourselves as butterflies fluttering over a cabbage patch.

Dylan saw me looking.

"She's practising her eurythmy," he said. I stared at him blankly, not a clue what he was talking about.

"Eurythmy. Beautiful, isn't it? It's an expressive form of dance. Comes from the soul. Very pure, very natural," he said, and smiled encouragingly, looking to see if I understood.

He explained that St. George's House was home to teachers from the local Rudolf Steiner school. I realised he was describing John's House, the school directly across the street from The Messenger.

I told him I worked for the paper, and his face instantly brightened, and he stepped back and bowed in an exaggerated gesture of courtly civility.

"Oh, come in, come in, we're neighbours. You're just in time to have some tea," he said. "The kettles on. I was just about to make some toast with honey."

"No, I need to get on," I said. "I have to find somewhere to live. My editor's given me the afternoon to find a place. He's counting on me coming back with good news."

I took a step back, and as I did, I was conscious that I had totally misjudged Dylan, and I felt ashamed for jumping to conclusions and thinking the worst, that he had been smoking marijuana. I realised he was just being kind and friendly. It was not the last time I would misjudge Dylan Bishop.

"Well, good luck," said Dylan. "I'm sure our paths will cross again. I'm up and down the hill all the time. We're bound to bump into one another."

I retraced my steps through the garden to the large main gate. As I walked alongside the house, I could see the dancer through a window, still leaping and whirling around, dropping to her knees and springing back up again, her arms moving gracefully up and down.

From George's House, it was only a short walk across the

town square to Market Street, where I was going to look at an old terraced house for rent.

The downpour had drenched the streets, washing them clean and leaving pavements shiny with mirror-like puddles in the gutters.

These dark pools pulled clouds to the ground and reflected the brick walls and roofs nearby, turning them into beautiful, upside-down pictures.

A mother with her young daughter hopped over a puddle in an elegant leap to reach the pavement without getting her feet wet. She reminded me of the girl practising eurythmy.

The ad in the paper said to ask Mrs. Dawes at No. 10 for the key. I knocked on the door of No. 10, and it was opened by a middle-aged woman who looked flustered and out of breath.

Before I had time to speak, she turned and yelled at children rough-housing inside to shut up and stop being naughty. She knew immediately why I was there and went and got the key, then returned and pointed me down the ginnel, a passageway, at the side between the two houses.

"This house was the home of a coal miner and his wife . They lived here all their life," said Mrs. Dawes. "He died from emphysema two years ago. His wife died a few months later, heartbroken, I reckon, after 50 years of marriage. I knew them all my life. I grew up here. They were like a mum and dad to me."

The house had been empty for months. It was being rented by the couple's son and his wife.

"They don't want to sell it," said Mrs. Dawes. "They didn't want to rent it, but they don't want to live here, either. They have no other family, so they asked if I would look after renting it out. It is too painful for them to do it."

She handed me the key and pointed to a high wooden gate that opened into a small, brick-paved courtyard. The key opened the door to the kitchen.

Inside, everything was spotless. Pots and pans were neatly

stacked on shelves. Cupboard contained rows of cups dangling from hooks and plates stacked in tidy piles.

The living room had an old settee, two easy chairs facing the fireplace, and a Welsh dresser in a corner. In the hearth, there was a full scuttle of coal, and pushed close to the window was an old dining table, partially covered by a white tablecloth placed in a diamond shape. In the centre of the table was an empty fruit bowl.

Daylight streamed in through the window, casting shadows on the fern-patterned wallpaper. I sank into an easy chair and looked at the empty fireplace.

In the silence and stillness, I felt I could fall asleep. The calm and quiet of the room felt so peaceful.

Suddenly, there was a noise at the window. A black cat had jumped the fence and was standing on the window ledge, looking in.

Mrs. Dawes appeared, shooed the cat away and tapped on the window to let me know she was there and was coming in.

"What d'you think?" she asked, looking pleased with how clean and tidy everything was.

"I like it. Very clean. And not too far from my office."

"Office?" said Mrs. Dawes.

"Yes, I'm with the Messenger, the new reporter."

"Oh, very good. That's nice," she said politely. "Have you seen upstairs? The bedrooms?" She opened a door and pointed up steep stairs.

"There are three, but you'll only need one. One is an attic room. Too small, really, for a bedroom."

I climbed the stairs and took a quick look inside each of the rooms. They were all tiny and unfurnished, with floors covered with linoleum.

When I came down, Mrs. Dawes was standing by the back door in the kitchen, waiting to lock up.

I told her I would like to move in as soon as possible. She said Saturday would be best as she had help with the kids that day. She locked the door behind us, and we walked up the passageway, me following closely behind her as she spoke, her words echoing in the brick tunnel.

"I will see you early Saturday then," she said, then turned, remembering something important. "Oh yes, I'll need the first week's rent on Saturday, too. Three pounds 15 shillings, right? I think it's a bargain considering how much space you have and a yard."

I nodded, smiled, thanked her, and watched as she disappeared into her house and closed the door.

I decided to catch the faster single-deck bus home. I liked the route better, along country lanes, through the village of Awesworth, into Kimberley, and then on into Eastwood, Nuthall and my home in Aspley.

All the way home, I thought about the house I had just rented, and how nice it would be to make a coal fire, close the curtains and have a place of my own for the first time.

* * *

CHAPTER FOURTEEN
PIGEONS

A flock of pigeons swooped fast and low over the dark roofs of terraced houses on Wilton Street.

The pigeons circled twice, gliding in a graceful cloud of perfect synchronisation, then dropped to land on the flat roof of a painted wooden loft in Sam Small's backyard.

I watched the birds from a distance as I made my way to find Sam's house. The birds appeared and disappeared, rising and falling, between the roofs of houses.

I had jotted down the address on a piece of paper. I knew the way to Wilton Street, but I liked the idea that the pigeons were looking out for me and wanted to guide me to the right house without my having to look at numbers.

On Wilton Street, I scanned the sky and saw the pigeons turn, swoop, dip and vanish behind a house in the middle of the row.

All the houses looked identical, each with a simple brick façade, black door, white doorstep, and windows with thick green ledges.

Outside the house, I looked at the number on the door. No. 16. I looked at the paper in my hand. No. 16.

I knocked, and a woman with a hairnet and carpet slippers

came to the door. She was drying her hands on a tea towel as she looked for me to explain who I was and what I wanted.

"I'm from the Messenger, to see Sam, to pick up his column," I said.

"He's out back, with the pigeons, at the loft," she said. "Go round, you'll find him. He's always at the loft."

I turned to make my way down the alley.

"I'm Vera, his wife," she called after me. "Just in case you come again."

She went back inside and slammed the front door.

Sam wrote a weekly column, Pigeon Notes, about pigeon racing and pigeon fanciers. Dan Wootton had asked me to pick up his latest column and give Sam a cheque for his past three pieces.

Sam saw me coming up the path well before I spotted him.

"Over here," he shouted. I waved and made my way to where he stood, carefully stepping around flower pots as I went.

Sam was a short, stout man in his 60s with a ruddy complexion that made me think he had spent one too many nights at the pub.

It also crossed my mind that he was probably the kind of man who liked to be out at the loft, caring for his pigeon, more than being in the house with Vera.

In his red-and-black chequered shirt and baggy trousers, he looked slightly comical like a slapstick comedian in a music hall act. It was a look that immediately made him more endearing to me rather than the opposite.

As I drew nearer, I noticed that he was waving his hands in the air as if conducting a brass band or a symphony orchestra. It turned out to be his vain attempt to get pigeons off the roof and into their nesting boxes.

"They're a bit nervous today. I'm not sure why," he said. "They don't want to go back in. They're probably wondering who you are and why you're here. Some are still in training. They're not settled. Not used to their bases yet. It takes a while."

I introduced myself, but he already knew who I was and why I was there.

"You've come for my column. I telephoned the Messenger yesterday to say I couldn't bring the column in myself. They said they'd send you."

I handed him the envelope containing a cheque for four pounds and ten shillings, thirty shillings for each of his previous columns.

He took the envelope, folded it into his pocket without looking at what was inside.

"It pays for feed," he said, gesturing at the birds, most of which had now entered the loft with one or two still fluttering hesitantly on the landing board.

"I don't do it for the money, write the column, you understand. I do it for the other fanciers. They like to read about the races and see their names in the paper."

Sam reached into a cage, gently grabbed a bird with iridescent green and purple colours on its neck, and he gently, expertly fanned its wings, spreading them to expose individual feathers.

"This is my best bird, Queenie," he said. "She's a champion. She's won me quite a few races."

He continued inspecting the wings, spreading the feathers and examining the structure closely. All the time, the bird rested calmly in his grip.

Sam's hands were rough and calloused, but he was as gentle with the bird as a mother holding a baby. He lifted Queenie closer to his face and looked admiringly into the bird's small, dark, nervous eyes.

"I worry about flying her now. Too many peregrines, too many sparrow-hawks. I'm scared she won't get back. We're losing too many birds these days. Every race, a few more don't make it back. Anyhow, I'm going to rest her and use her only for breeding. Her racing days are over. Who knows, maybe she'll give me a champion."

"I know nothing about pigeons," I told him.

"That's okay. Neither did I once upon a time."

"I've seen pigeons in the Market Square in Nottingham," I said. "When I was a kid, I even took breadcrumbs to feed them."

"Those aren't racing pigeons," said Sam indignantly. "My birds are special, bred to fly long distances and make it back home as fast as they can, in record time. These are intelligent pigeons, not like the ones in Market Square. These birds can fly 100 miles an hour. Imagine that."

He looked proudly at the birds cooing in the loft behind a screen of chicken wire. I tried to see what it was Sam admired about them. For the first time, I noticed variations in colours. Some birds were more white than grey, others were almost black. A few had spots or speckles. One was cappuccino brown.

"These are the thoroughbreds of the sky," said Sam. "They fly through wind and rain. They travel hundreds of miles, never stopping, well, perhaps they stop once for a sip of water, but they always keep going, they never give up. They have great courage."

'Courage!" I guffawed cynically. "I never thought of a pigeon as having courage."

Sam shook his head at my ignorance and looked sternly at me, but with an expression more of disappointment than anger.

"When a peregrine attacks, these birds don't give up. They can't give up. They keep flying. They keep trying to get home. Sometimes their wings get ripped and torn. Peregrines can be savage. But a good racing pigeon will keep going. I call that courage."

He walked away, shaking his head. I thought I had offended him and he was walking away in disgust, then he stopped, turned and said, "Wait here, I'll be back. I'm just going to get my column."

He returned holding two crumpled pieces of paper on which were written words, barely legible, scribbled in blue ballpoint. I took the papers and looked more closely. Some words were pale, hard-to-read, ghostly outlines, others were bold and easy to read. The ballpoint had clearly been working only intermittently.

There were numerous corrections in the margins. Words had been crossed out and replaced by other words, and sentences were squeezed in between lines, probably as an afterthought, and there were little arrows indicating where the added sentences were supposed to go.

I frowned, my eyebrows jumping up and down, trying to make sense of the jumbled text. I looked up at Sam and smiled weakly. He read my thoughts and knew exactly what I was thinking, and he shrugged and shot me an apologetic look of helpless resignation.

"You have to make sense of it," he said. "That's how we've always done it. I just give you my notes, you do the rest. I write it, you type it. That's how we've always done it."

Vera arrived with two steaming mugs of tea. Sam looked at me and smiled as if we had just won a prize.

"I already put in milk and two sugars. Hope that's okay," she said, handing us each a mug before quickly turning, not waiting for a response.

"I've been racing pigeons for years," said Sam. "I worked down the pit at Shipley. Started there as a kid. It was tough. I got a bit depressed with it all. The birds saved me, they gave me a lift."

"Is it a lot of work, keeping pigeon?" I asked, sipping my tea and finding it still too hot. "Looks pretty messy."

"I don't care about that," said Sam. "It gives me something to do. I keep a clean loft. You have to, or the birds get sick. I can't have that."

He sipped his tea and looked affectionately at the pigeons in the loft.

"I used to drink quite a bit. I was down the pub every night. But when I got the pigeons, I stopped going to the pub and I stopped drinking altogether. I just didn't like it anymore. Funny that."

A woman in the yard next door began hanging out washing. She came to the fence, and looked over to see who Sam was talking to. Sam said nothing, just nodded. She studied us both, took a good, long look at me, then went back to pegging clothes on the line.

"Don't the neighbours mind, Sam? All the mess from the birds?" I asked.

"There's no mess. I told you. I clean it up. It's never a problem. Neighbours don't care. They know it's what we do around here. They like the birds just as I do. They like to see them flying.

"You want to know the best part. The best part is when a bird comes home. When a bird comes in, I could jump for joy. It's a fantastic feeling."

"Fantastic?" I said with obvious scepticism.

"Oh yes, it's a big thrill, especially when they've come all the way from Scotland or North Yorkshire. Do you know how far that is? It's far. And to think they get here so fast. It's fantastic."

Sam pulled the lid off a plastic bucket, scooped out a mix of seeds, and filled some of the feed boxes in the loft. Satisfied, he grabbed his mug of tea, took a sip and smiled contently at me.

"I painted my loft with bright colours. It's like a welcome-home sign," he says. "I have 30 birds now. I used to have more. You always lose a few. They lose their way or get picked off by falcons."

"Who reads your column, Sam?" I asked.

"Fanciers like me. There are a lot of us. Mostly colliers. Some publicans have lofts. Ironworkers at Stapleton keep pigeons, too.

"I have to be here for the birds. I can't just feed 'em and forget 'em. That's why I can't go away on holiday. Vera hates it, but I tell her, I have to be here for the birds. She goes on her own now, to her sister's at Mablethorpe."

Sam picked up a wooden box with a sturdy leather handle and a clock face on the side.

"Pigeon racing is all about the time it takes for birds to get home. They get liberated, and the clock starts ticking.

"This is my time clock. As soon as a bird gets back, I take the rubber ring off its foot and put it in here to register the time. Then, it's official. That's how we know how long it took them, how fast they flew, and it's how we know which bird was first? You can't cheat, it's all recorded."

Sam looked into the loft.

"See that bird. It got back from Scotland in record time, but I couldn't get him to drop down. He just wouldn't settle. I was so mad. Then, I thought, maybe he's teaching me a lesson, not to take it all so seriously."

I looked questioningly at Sam.

"Probably not," he laughed.

I finished my tea and handed Sam the mug,

"This is my last column till we start again in April. Then, we go through to September. "

Sam was right. I ended up typing out his column, week after week. It was frustrating, sometimes impossible, to decipher his scrawl. And I groaned when I was forced to trust his terminology, not knowing what he was talking about, especially when he went on about rollers, squeakers, bibs, yearlings, droppers, day birds, tripping, traps, and time clock checks.

What kept me going was knowing how much Sam loved his birds.

* * *

CHAPTER FIFTEEN
ASSIGNMENT

Back to the office, everyone was in a buoyant mood and bursting with questions for me.

"Do you have a girlfriend," asked Brenda.

"No," I said. "Do you have someone in mind?" I asked.

"Are you still having problems remember the bus numbers?" asked Mrs. Partridge. "You should practice remembering telephone numbers. That'll help."

"I'm not having problems," I said. "I never forget. My memory's perfect."

"Is Sam Small over the infection he picked up from his birds?" Dan asked.

My eyes widened. Oh no, Sam has an infection? Before I could say a word, Ron handed me a cup of tea.

"You're with me in court tomorrow morning," he said. "Magistrates' court. You'll sit with me so I can show you the ropes."

"Oh joy!" mocked Matthew, and Ron shot him a dismissive look.

"Now, now, Matthew," said Dan. "You know you had to do it. And look how well that worked out."

Everyone laughed.

Apparently, Matthew had been banned from court for not being presentable. The clerk of the court took offence to his slovenly appearance and complained to Miss Marlowe. She took a very dim of Matthew's slovenliness.

She ordered Dan to keep him out of court for a month and insisted that he only be allowed to cover parish councils until he cleaned up his act and came to work looking tidier.

Mr Watson ignored everything that was going on and stayed at his desk, quietly munching on the second half of his beetroot sandwich.

The rest of us stood chatting and sipping our tea, warming our backsides against the stove.

"Harold, come and get your tea before it gets cold," Mrs. Partridge said, scolding his for ignoring us.

He shrugged, grunted something none of us could make out, and lumbered out of his chair and plodded like a grumpy polar bear to get his cup of tea.

I could never tell whether it was shyness or chronic melancholy that made him the way he was. I assumed it was a bit of both.

He was kind and courteous to Mrs. Partridge. He would never say or do anything to offend her. But he also struck me as hell bent on maintaining his image as an over-worked, world-weariness, grumpy pessimist. How this helped him make friends or keep friends or even have friends was a mystery to me.

As I started typing Sam's pigeon notes, Mrs. Partridge called for coke. I grabbed the shuttle and made for the door. Matthew jumped up and followed quickly behind me and pulled me away to go for a fried-egg sandwich. I put up no defence.

Stan was his unusual charming self.

"Oh fuck, look what the cat's dragged in," he said. "What the fuck do you two numbskulls want? Wasting my time again."

"Miss Marlowe sends her very good wishes, Stanley," said Matthew.

"Did she really?" asked Stan, genuinely excited that Miss

Marlowe might have mentioned him.

"Of course, Stanley. You know you are always uppermost in her thoughts. A man of your breeding and good character."

"Fuck off!" said Stan, irritated at being teased. "Now you get nothing. Bugger off!"

"Oh, please, Stanley. I'm sorry. I promise to mention you to Molly Marlowe. Honestly. The next time I see her. I'll tell her how kind and generous you and how you always look after her and make us the best sandwiches. Promise, Stan. And that goes for my partner here, too."

Stan relented and made us both our fried egg sandwiches. They were as delicious as ever. Who could explain why they tasted so good. We gobbled them down like a couple of hungry savages.

Matthew pulled me again from going down the alleyway to get coke.

"You shouldn't listen to Dan. He doesn't know as much as he'd like to you think. And Ron's no better. They're both a couple of hacks. Why would they be working here if there were any good.

"And don't let Partridge and Watson upset you. They're old and grumpy and they can be mean. They think they know everything but they know nothing.

"Anyway, I won't have to put up with all this much longer. I've applied for a new job and I reckon I'll get it. It's in Mansfield with a much bigger, better paper. You know Dan's looking for a new job, too. He'll be gone soon, you'll see."

"What? Dan is leaving?" I said.

"Oh no, I wasn't supposed to say anything," said Matthew. "He wants to go to Eastbourne. He's got a sister there. He wants a live by the sea. He wants quiet life in a prettier town. Promise me, you won't say a word."

Matthew went back into the office. I continue on to the coke pile in the backyard. As I rammed the scuttle deep into the pile, I caught a glimpse of Miss Marlowe in her sitting room. She was reading 'What It's Like to Die," the book I had seen on a chair at my interview.

I put the scuttle down and stared at her through the window, noticing how engrossed she was in the book.

Feeling my eyes on her, she looked up, caught me staring, smiled and gave a kind wave. I waved and jumped back and hurriedly filled the scuttle.

"Where've you been?" snapped Mrs. Partridge. "There's a parcel that needs to go to the printer. Come on, you'd better get going!"

Brenda smiled smugly, amused that I had been reprimanded. I showed her my teeth.

Back from the parcel drop, I continued typing the Pigeon Notes, squinting as I tried to make sense of Sam's awful handwriting. Dan stopped me mid-flow, as I ratter-tat-tatted away at my dressing table.

"Let's talk about some basic style rules. When you're writing a story, I want you to think of the length in terms of the number of paragraphs."

He held up a copy of the paper and pointed at the paragraphs in a story, pausing at each indent.

"You see this story, it has a total of six paragraphs. The introductions, an explanation, some detail, and a conclusion. Most stories can be told in six or eight paragraphs.

"Remember to start each paragraph with a different word. Never use the same word. For instance, Don't start every time paragraph with word 'the'. It looks odd in type. It's also repetitive and boring."

He grabbed one of my football reports off his desk and drew a circle around the first word of each paragraph.

"See, you've done exactly that here. You've started every new paragraph with the word 'the'. Don't do that.

"Your introduction, the first paragraph of the story, is also far too long," he said. "It shouldn't be more than 30 words.

"In fact, keep all your sentences short and sweet. They

should be no more than an alphabet and a half long in length, about 40 characters.

"Think of 'the quick brown fox jumps over the lazy dog.' That's 35 characters. I like intros that are short and to the point. Try to be concise and get to the point as quickly as possible."

He went through my football report, ringing words, crossing out paragraphs, switching sentences around. It was again a mass of red ink when he had finished.

"You need to put the most important, most interesting piece of information, right at the top, in your first paragraph, in the intro.

"You want to grab the reader's attention right from the start. If you write a boring intro, you can't expect readers to stay with you and keep reading. Okay, that's enough for now."

When I finished the Pigeon Notes, Dan sent me on my first out-of-office assignment to the village of Awesworth to interview a former coal miner, Arthur Hutchinson, who had overcome chronic depression by learning to paint pictures of landscapes, flowers, and scenes around his village.

Dan said Hutchinson's story was about the miracle of transformation, how someone went from despair to happiness, darkness to light, by learning to paint and learning to believe in something positive again.

"Get his story. Let him tell you how painting has changed his life for the better," said Dan.

Hutchinson told me all about his nervous breakdown. He had become more and more depressed working as a miner down the pit.

"One day everything went dark and black and I felt like killing himself," he said.

He told me how oil painting, making pictures of flowers and country scenes, changed everything.

"It was something I loved doing when I was a kid at school," he told me. "I never thought I could do it again. It has changed my life. I'm happy now, never been happier."

Dan liked my finished story.

"You got a lot good information in here. That's good. People want to know everything. I like that you said he knows nothing about the theory of art or art history.

"People love to read about amateurs who are as good as professionals. No one likes a know it all.

"And I like how you connected his art to his illness when you say 'the scenes and moods he creates in his painting often reflect the loneliness and isolation he felt during his illness'.

"Readers will like that. They like it when you show empathy, when you show you care and understand how other people feel and the pain they are going through."

I felt pleased with myself, but then Dan said, "The only thing missing is Arthur's voice."

"His voice?" I asked.

"Yes, his voice. I can't hear your voice. I hear you talking about him. I hear you saying how hard it was for him, what painting has done for him, how much better he feeling, but I don't hear him saying any of these things. Nothing. Where's his voice. Where are the quotes?"

"Quotes?" I asked.

"Yes, you have to let people speak for themselves, use his own words, let them be heard in their own words so we can hear their voice.

"And you need to get it right. Don't make it up. Don't write what you think he said or what you think he might have said. It needs to be precise, in his own words, the way he speaks, the way he said it.

"Remember, there's power in the spoken word. We need to listen carefully, then accurately write down what people say, and report exactly what they say. It's important. Always let people speak for themselves."

* * *

CHAPTER SIXTEEN
COURT

The magistrates' court was held once a week, every Thursday, at the town hall in the main room, which was also used for concerts, ceremonies, wedding parties, and other special events.

Portraits of former mayors lined the walls, and the old dark wood panelling gave the room a dry, fusty smell like a church with old pews.

Ron and I sat next to one another at a plain table set at a right angle to the large, imposing, formal desk for the magistrates.

Peter, from the Telegraph, and Rory, from the Post, were already in their seats. They were sharing a joke and giggling like schoolboys. Ron shot them a dismissive look. I could see he thought this was a time to be quiet and show respect.

At 10 o'clock sharp, three magistrates paraded in and took their places. Head magistrate was Mrs Maggie Vincent, a beautiful blonde in her mid-40s, a popular Liberal town councillor and the wife of a local doctor. Intelligent, stylish and fearless, she had the looks of a supermodel and the presence of an opera diva.

Everyone at the Press table was in love with her, even lusted after her. She was gorgeous, and everyone, including righteous

Ron, stared at her in awe and admiration. She smiled at us when she entered. We smiled back at her with dreamy eyes and goofy grins.

The clerk of the court called out, Ronald Webster, the first name of the docket.

"It's due care and attention," Ron whispered, pointing at the charge sheet.

"Bet he's driven into the back of someone or smashed into a road sign or something stupid like that. He'll get a 15 quid fine, 10 if he's lucky."

The clerk told the court that Webster, a local shopkeeper, was "not paying sufficient attention" when he drove along High Lane East and collided with a parked lorry, injuring himself and putting a dent in the side of the lorry.

"Mr Webster has pleaded guilty," the clerk told the bench. "It's his first offence."

Mrs Vincent consulted with her colleagues, then announced that Webster would be fined 15 pounds and given a three-month driving suspension.

She looked directly at the Press table as she announced her decision. We smiled back, grateful for the recognition, glad, in fact, of any attention she deemed to bestow on us, and delighted to have the opportunity to flirt and show her how we all adored her.

Ron wrote down the fine on his court sheet, and the clerk called the next name on the list. From that point, the proceedings galloped along at a much quicker pace.

George Bradwell was fined 20 pounds for using a goods vehicle without a Goods Vehicle Test Certificate.

Roy Bandy, a bus inspector, was fined 15 pounds for driving without due care and attention when he was in "collision with a mini-bus" taking pensioners to a bingo night.

Fines were handed out for not having a test certificate, driving without insurance, driving without a licence, dangerous driving, and for being a learner and carrying an unqualified passenger on a motorcycle.

Ron wrote down everything on the charge sheet.

"This is all minor stuff," Ron whispered. "But readers like it. Names sell newspapers. That's what Miss Marlowe always says. She likes to see as many names in the paper as possible.

"I once told her, 'Well, if names are so important, why don't we just publish the telephone directory?' She gave me such a withering look, I found myself apologising for my stupidity immediately."

Following a short adjournment, the magistrates returned. Mrs Vincent looked as calm and collected as ever, without a trace of fatigue or weariness. Cases were more complicated, more serious and a lot more interesting.

Two young men, accused of stealing lead from the roof of St. John's, were fined 25 pounds each and put on probation for two years.

"When police caught them red-handed, they denied stealing the lead," said the court clerk. "They claimed they had just found the lead lying there on the ground and thought it had been dumped and belonged to no one.

"However, they had no explanation for the ladder and all the tools in the two large bags they were carrying," he added.

Mrs Vincent rolled her eyes, clearly offended by the incompetence of the pair as much as by their stupidity. All of us at the press table snickered.

Joseph Peters, an out-of-work labourer, was fined 25 pounds for breaking and entering after being caught with items stolen from the police station.

"The defendant broke into the station and stole his own criminal records from a filing cabinet in a side office," said the clerk.

"Officers found a side window broken and the office ransacked. When they checked for missing items, they discovered files about Peters had been taken.

"They went straight away to Peters' home in Cotmanhay, where the defender was found alone in the kitchen, reading the details of his past crimes."

The saddest case of the day was that of Dorothy Jones, the wife of the headmaster of Blackstone secondary school, who was accused of shoplifting, stealing soap, shampoo and perfume from Boots the chemist.

She appeared in person, pleaded guilty, and was fined 15 pounds and given a conditional discharge.

"I am so sorry," she told the court. "I was confused at the time. I intended to pay for the items, but forgot. I don't know what happened. I just walked out without paying. I felt so ashamed."

The clerk jumped to his feet and addressed the bench.

"When she was apprehended, the defendant offered to pay for the items, but the store's manager, a Miss Shirley Meeker, refused her offer and insisted on calling the police.

"Apparently, Miss Meeker insisted that the police arrest and charge Mrs. Jones, something they felt obliged to do rather than send her home with a caution.

"We have since learned that Miss Meeker was a pupil at Blackstone school and she and her family had numerous confrontations with Mrs Jones's husband, who is the headmaster."

The court was silent. Mrs. Jones stood alone in the courtroom, on the verge of tears, and looked very sad, alone and vulnerable in her pillbox hat and sage green coat.

Mr. Jones sat at the back of the court. He was not allowed to stand by his wife, who was pale and trembling and looked the very definition of a polite, conservative, middle-class housewife.

The court seemed to view her in the same light. She had made a mistake and appeared genuinely sorry for what she had done.

Mrs Vincent was the first to speak as she handed out the sentence. Her voice was calm and compassionate.

"Mrs. Jones, we want you to know that the court sympathises with your predicament and understands how easily such a thing can happen.

"We want you to go away from here with confidence, knowing that you have faced this charge with dignity and composure. You have been honest and forthright. For that, we thank you very much.

"But please, Mrs Jones, let this be the last of it. None of us want to see you here before us again. Is that understood?"

Mrs Jones nodded, pulled a handkerchief from her handbag and dabbed her eyes. She turned, muttering 'Thank you, thank you' and walked quickly to her husband. He put his arm around her and left the courtroom together.

By noon, the proceedings were over. Mrs Vincent stood up, smiled at the Press table, and left, followed closely by the other magistrates.

Ron and I walked quickly back to the office.

"This is the only day we have a real deadline," said Ron. "We need to get copy out fast and off to the printers. There's no time to lose."

"Can you write that fast?" I said as we dodged around people on the pavement.

"Yes, you don't have much time to think about it. You just have to rattle it out. It's easy stuff. Get the name, the charge, the plea and the fine. Three or four paragraphs max on each one. You'll get the hang of it."

Back at the office, Ron dropped his coat over the back of his chair and began pounding away at his typewriter.

Dan popped by every few minutes to pick up Ron's copy. He edited it quickly, making tick marks at the end of each paragraph.

I was impressed by how few changes he made. Within an hour, Ron was finished. All his copy was stuffed into a parcel, and I was dispatched to the bus stop to send it on its way.

The afternoon rolled on. Matthew appeared and disappeared.

Mr Watson went out, came back, and went out again. Mrs. Partridge called for more coke. Brenda lost her temper with someone on the phone and screamed out of frustration. Dan Wootton left to go to the printers. He would remain there until after midnight, until the paper was finally put to bed.

* * *

CHAPTER SEVENTEEN
FRIDAY

Bundles of papers, bound by plastic bands, were piled up in the office doorway when I arrived Friday morning.

Mrs. Partridge appeared, rummaged through her handbag for the key, opened the door, and Brenda pushed past her before she could retrieve the key from the lock.

"Charming!" said Mrs Partridge, sarcastically rebuking Brenda for her rudeness.

I carried in the bundles of papers, and Brenda cut the string, binding them, and we all grabbed a copy of the latest edition of the Chesterton Messenger and Irremor Valley Journal.

I flipped the pages to find the stories I had written and immediately spotted the wedding reports, football reports, the Pigeon News, and my interview with Arthur Hutchinson. The story ran with a photo of Hutchinson smiling and holding one of his landscape paintings.

Ron's story about Mrs Jones, the shoplifter, filled the top of page 3. The headline read: Headmaster's wife guilty of theft. I thought it sounded a little harsh, especially when I thought back to how sad and forlorn she looked in court the day before.

But I read Ron's story, and it was totally accurate. He had not said anything more than what was said in court. He had even added the detail about Mrs Jones offering to pay and how the shop manager refused to allow her, and instead insisted on the police arresting her and charging her with shoplifting. It seemed to balance the harshness of her disgrace in court.

Brenda came and dropped a large brown envelope on the desk in front of me.

"Photos," she announced abruptly. "For the window."

I looked at her blankly.

"Come with me," she demanded, and I dutifully followed her into the cramped cubbyhole that was Matthew's corner workspace.

Brenda twisted two metal latches to release the black backdrop screen from the front display window.

"There you go. Pin the photos here. Take out last week's old ones, put in this week's new ones."

She handed me the brown envelope and smiled mischievously as she walked back to her desk.

Inside the envelope, I found all the original black-and-white photos from the latest edition of the paper. Wedding photos. Pictures of brides and bridesmaids, grooms and groomsmen. Football photos, all action shots, and one or two with trophies or shields being held up.

There were photos of the mayor presenting a cheque at the hospital, and photos of Arthur Hutchinson with his paintings.

I pulled the old photos off the board and pinned the new ones in place. As I worked, people walking by stopped to stare. I held up pictures I was about to pin to show them through the window. They nodded and grinned happily, grateful for my show of courtesy.

When the picture window was done, I started to move back to my desk, but Brenda saw me and shouted, "Okay, now it's time for you to do wrappers."

"Wrappers?" I asked.

"Yes, we wrap and mail papers to ex-Chestertonians all over

the world. They are people who've emigrated but still want the paper to find out what's going on in the old town."

Brenda handed me a sheath of wrappers, all with addresses already printed on them. She picked up a paper, grabbed a wrapper, quickly rolled it around the paper, then snapped a strip of cellotape to seal the join, and dropped the wrapped paper into a cardboard box.

"There you go," she said. "That's how you do it. Now you do the rest. It's all part of your job."

I got the feeling she liked reminding me that I was not important, even if I was technically being called a reporter.

Papers were sent all over the world, to Chestertonians now living in Canada, New Zealand, Australia, and South Africa, as well as to other parts of England, such as Cornwall, the Scilly Isles, the Channel Islands, and up north to parts of Yorkshire, Lancashire and Scotland.

"Mr. Tom Wallace, Brisbane, Australia," I said, reading a wrapper. "Where's Brisbane?"

"North of Sydney," said Mrs. Partridge, speaking quickly and with confidence.

"Newcastle, Australia? There's a Newcastle in Australia."

"Yes, and a Perth," said Brenda. "And a South Wales, well, a New South Wales."

I was intrigued by other place names on the wrappers. Hamilton, Ontario. Dunedin, New Zealand. Medicine Hat, Alberta.

"Where's Adelaide?" I asked.

"Southern Australia, A good distance west of Sydney," said Mrs. Partridge.

"These people sometimes come back to visit. If we know about it, somebody usually tells us, we interview them, ask them about their new life in Australia or Canada. It's always interesting. Readers like it. Most of migrants say they're glad they left."

Wrapping the papers took a long time, twice as long as

pinning photos in the window, and much more exhausting and monotonous.

But Friday was a fun day, a time to relax after the stresses of the week and get ready for the weekend. Brenda and Mrs Partridge were more friendly and chatty, and even Mr Watson seemed in a brighter, more cheery mood.

Dan never came in on Fridays as he had been up until after midnight at the printers. Ron was also never in on a Friday because he was working the next day, covering the Chesterton Town football game.

Matthew was supposed to be in on time, but never was. He always showed up later, knowing Dan would not be there. This day, he arrived and quickly excused himself and disappeared to get a sandwich at Stan's.

Mrs. Partridge assumed control of the office in Dan Wootton's absence, and she told me, with great pomp and authority, that I could leave at noon, since I was working on Saturday.

"I'm working tomorrow?" I said, surprised.

"Oh yes," she said. "Didn't you check the diary?"

I looked at the clipboard, and there was my name next to a list of church events. Bake sale at St. Bartholomew's, Hallam Fields. Fundraiser at South Street Baptist. Rummage sale at Ebenezer Methodist on Charlotte Street.

Matthew stepped back into the office, just in time to hear our conversation and see me looking at the diary.

"Make sure you get all the names," he said. "We like names. Get every name of every person at every stall." He smirked, knowing how dreary it all sounded.

"And remember to ask the organisers to phone you first thing on Monday about the total amount raised. Leave that out and you won't hear the last of it."

As I was about to leave, Mr Watson came up and handed me a small brown envelope.

"Your first week's wages," he said.

On the envelope was a breakdown of the contents, showing

the total amount inside, minus tax and insurance. The total came to twelve pounds, fifteen shillings, all in cash.

The paper money was neatly folded, and the coins added weight and bulk to the envelope. I returned the money into the envelope, grabbed my coat, said my goodbyes and left. That was the end of my first week at the Messenger.

CHAPTER EIGHTEEN
SATURDAY

I arrived early Saturday morning to pick up the key from Mrs. Dawes for the terraced house I rented.

With a bag of groceries in one hand and a suitcase of clothes in the other, I lumbered clumsily up to the front door, knocked and waited for her to answer.

It was cold and blustery, and all I could think about was getting inside, out of the wind, into my new home, and having a cup of tea and some breakfast.

Mrs Dawes took her time to answer. There was a commotion going on inside. When she finally opened the door, she dashed back inside and shouted at kids to clean up their mess and stop buggering around, then she returned, pressing the key into my hand.

"Sorry, I can't stand and chat. My kids are driving me nuts." She pointed me down the alleyway, smiled, and closed the door.

A second later, the door flew open again, and Mrs Dawes shouted after me.

"I'll get the rent later, or you can pop it in an envelope and put it through the letterbox."

Inside my new lodgings, I immediately set about making a

coal fire, something I was quite expert at, having had to make one every day after school before my mother came home from work.

My process was never changed. I took pages of a newspaper, rolled them into long, slender tubes, then carefully folded the tubes around my hand to form a spill. This time, I used the latest edition of The Messenger. I had packed several copies.

As I rolled each spill, I could see the stories, some of which I had written. There was Matthew's report on the Trowell parish council, Ron's court report about the thieves who stole lead from the church roof, and Dan's story about a new council project to build more houses. I rolled Sam Small's Pigeon Notes and scrunched up the page containing all my wedding reports.

At first, I hesitated to use these stories to make a fire. It felt wrong, considering all the work I knew had gone into writing them.

Then, the thought crossed my mind that it was all yesterday's news and there would be many more stories to write.

I continued rolling the paper and setting the spills in layers in the grate and began precisely placing small chunks of coal on top, ensuring each piece was in the best position to catch alight and then pass its heat to the chunk of coal beside it.

I regarded making a quality coal fire a precise art that involved patience, skilful construction and expert timing.

Once the first spill was lit, I sat back and watched flames grow and spread, igniting other spills. The black nuggets of coal quickly caught fire and turned the whole heap into a cracking, popping, snapping mound of dancing red and yellow flames. I found the sight mesmerising.

I watched Ron's court story go up in flames. My football reports went up in a flash and turned into ash in seconds. One by one, all the stories vanished in flames.

I had never watched a fire so closely or intently. I imagined The Messenger being used in a similar way in homes all over the town. The thought made me smile. Instead of finding the idea alarming or disappointing,

I liked the notion that our stories not only gave people news and important information but also brought warmth to their homes and took the chill out of the air.

I watched the fire grow, as one blazing coal slowly passed its heat to another, and the little fiery mound glowed and filled the little living room with warmth and light.

I began unpacking, placing books on the mantlepiece, shirts in the drawers of the Welsh dresser, and my suit and raincoat in the hall closet.

From the grocery bag, I took out a bottle of milk, sliced bread, a tub of butter, a tin of tea, a jar of honey, a half dozen eggs, and a box of Cornflakes.

The fridge in the kitchen was working well, cold and humming with a super bright light that came on whenever the door was opened, and there was ample shelf space in cupboards for the rest of my groceries. I felt accomplished when everything was in its rightful place.

My breakfasts, I had decided, would consist of cereal and toast and a cup of tea, perhaps a boiled egg. I knew I was capable of assembling all of that without any fuss.

As for dinner, I had it in mind to boil potatoes, peas, and carrots, and fry a pork chop or some pork sausages. Fish and chips, I knew I could buy any time from the local chippy.

As I did all this, Rory's words rang in my ears about the value of getting free food at Press receptions. The thought made me smile. I hoped it was true.

In the living room, the fire was crackling beautifully. I thought it looked beautiful as the coals glowed and crumbled with small blue and yellow flames licking up from the bed of red embers.

In silence, broken only by the sound of the fire, I made a pot of tea, buttered toast with honey, and sat, happy to watch flames flickering in the fireplace.

My afternoon was spent going to all the church bazaars, fetes and fundraisers I was down on the diary to cover.

Before leaving and locking up the house, I added more chunks of coal to the fire, then dampened it down with a sprinkling of dusty slack. I knew this would slow it down and make it last, if I was lucky, until I returned.

In front of the hearth, I placed an old, tarnished, golden fire guard that resembled a large fencing mask. It fit perfectly, covering the grate. I knew it would stop any pops, snaps, and sparks leaping from the fire onto the carpet.

At the church functions, I did precisely as Matthew had advised and wrote down the name of every person in charge of every stall or booth.

There were a lot of stalls: tombola, lucky dip, silent auction, knitted items, cake stand, and always a tea and refreshments table.

As I jotted down names, I made a point of asking each person to spell their name, just to ensure that I got it right. I soon discovered there was more than one way to spell even the most common names.

There was Ann and Ann with an 'e', Sarah with an 'h', and Sara with no 'h'. As I jotted down the names, the person would look over my shoulder and correct me as I wrote.

Not Amy, it's Aimee, A I M E E.

Not Sheila, Shelagh.

Not Cathrine, it's Kathryn.

Leslie, not Lesley.

Sean, not Shawn.

It was all new to me. A lesson in how differently a name could be spelt. I was glad of the correction. Nevertheless, it was exhausting and humbling to be so wrong, so often, despite my best efforts to get it right first time. No matter how I apologised, there was always a lingering element of irritation from the offended person as if I ought to have known better.

Every event had a coordinator, a treasurer, a secretary, or a head of committee who absolutely had to "get a mention."

Stalls, I discovered, were never ever run by one person; it was always a team of two, three or four. And everyone had to be mentioned.

Bits and Bobs was a table filled with tea cups, milk jugs, flower vases, fruit bowls, tea caddies and rosy-patterned biscuit tins.

Odds and Sorts sounded the same, but it was not. It was a table containing a jumble of salt and pepper shakers, porcelain figurines, magnifying glasses, and mismatched sets of silver cutlery.

The Knitted Goods table offers homemade gloves, scarves, and baby blankets. The Treasure Hunt was a sand pit where you placed a marker and hoped to win a buried prize.

The Bric-a-Brac stall offered stacks of dusty, old books, faded magazines, old photographs, records, drawings and paintings by amateur artists of birds, flowers, and landscape scenes.

Before leaving, I made sure to give my name and phone number to the person in charge. My contact information was always taken with great respect, followed by an earnest promise to call me first thing Monday to let me know the total amount raised.

The interest I showed was always returned in equal enthusiasm, and with a touching gesture of appreciation and gratitude. I was given biscuits, muffins, and homemade bread to take home. I ended up having to refuse because my hands were full, it was too much to carry.

It was dark by the time I headed home. The streets were emptying, and lights were coming on. A gust of wind lifted a page of The Messenger from the pavement and the page floated and flapped like a big bird into an empty shop doorway.

I patted my pocket to check that my notebook was still safe. I thought about all the faces I had looked into, all the names I had written down, all the hellos and handshakes and pats-on-the-back I had received.

I felt good when it was all over. It felt like I had done important, meaningful work —something that mattered.

It made me happy to think that the names I had written down would be in the paper next week and would be read by friends gathered together in church halls and church basements.

When I got home, the fire was out.

* * *

CHAPTER NINETEEN
GIFTS

'Don't use the word Xmas," said Dan. "Readers hate it when we call it Xmas. They phone. They write letters. 'It's Christmas, not Xmas,' they say. And they insist on it."

In the weeks leading up to Christmas, I was given the job of compiling notices of all upcoming festive events: concerts, banquets, pageants, and New Year's celebrations.

Notices flooded it by the bucketload. Our mail sack was heavy and bulging every day, twice its normal weight.

Brenda sorted through the avalanche of publicity requests, ripping open envelope after envelope with her dagger-like letter opener.

In no time at all, she had two shifting, spilling piles of paper, one consisting of torn envelopes, ready to be tossed into the wastepaper basket, the other, a fluid slipping mound of leaflets, letters and invitations for a myriad of upcoming festivities, a cornucopia of celebrations, everything from school concerts to carol services to nativity plays.

Brenda dumped all these Press releases on Dan's desk, and he quickly moved them onto the desk, where I was already madly typing away, creating one long story, the title of which was yet to be decided, possibly Our Merry Christmas Calendar or Your Guide to Christmas Fun.

Mrs Partridge and Brenda put up decorations. They pinned red and green paper garlands around the edges of desks, over doors, and around windows, with tiny sprigs of holly tucked into corners.

Christmas cards came pouring in from faithful advertisers, grateful readers, service clubs, charity clubs, councils and associations.

Brenda took it upon herself to curate the entire collection before deciding which cards were worth displaying. There was a vast assortment of seasonal images from plump Santas, robins and reindeer to ice-skaters on mirror-ponds and Christmas trees with baubles.

Brenda's favourites, ones she deemed worthy of pinning up, showed fireplaces with stockings hung with care, reindeer pulling Santa on his sleigh and Dickensian carollers.

She was also partial to cards depicting angels singing, wise men arriving, shepherds watching, the Bethlehem star shining, and any kind of nativity scenes, especially ones with a heavenly, sun-yellow light radiating from the manger.

Bottom of Brenda's list were all the vague, generic, ambiguous greeting cards, particularly ones proclaiming Happy Holidays or Season's Greetings, or ones with one-word, LOVE, JOY, PEACE, HOPE, especially ones with the word superimposed on a textured silver, red or golden background.

Outside, it was cold and the pavements were white with frost. But in the office, heat from the coke stove baked us like biscuits in an oven.

The door often burst open and people would come tumbling in, frozen, shivering and gasping for relief from the bone-chilling air, glad to find themselves in the warmth of our toasty little hothouse.

On the counter, next to Brenda, was a tray of home-baked biscuits, each one in the shape of a Christmas tree, snowflake, half-moon or five-pointed star. These were circled by a necklace of crumbly, open-topped mince-pies, all lightly dusted with icing sugar.

Next to the tray was an open box of milk chocolates, a gift to the office from Matthews' mother, along with a bowl of satsumas, heaped into a pyramid.

Before stepping back into the cold, customers were invited to help themselves to one of the goodies on display. Mrs. Partridge found it impossible to resist making a recommendation, endorsing the superiority of home-baking over store-bought chocolates, and always insisting people take a satsuma for their pocket.

The town loved Christmas. A tall fir tree was put up and decorated in the market square. Shops on Bath Street made every effort to decorate windows with festive signs and images. Some even hired a local artist to paint wintery scenes depicting Father Christmas delivering presents, angels singing or a jolly Rudolph the Reindeer with a bright red nose.

The cake shop was always popular, not only for the mouthwatering cakes, breads, buns and biscuits for sale, but for the incredible delicious smell of hot mince pies and sausage rolls fresh from the oven.

Matthew was a regular customer. He often turned up holding a bag of hot sausage rolls to share with the rest of us, something that made up for his perpetual lateness and inexplicable absences.

It was traditional for Mr Watson to walk the town at Christmas, stopping at shops and stores that had advertised during the year, to thank them for their business.

What he was really doing was calling to collect his Christmas bounty. All the shopkeepers knew the drill. Harold's visit never came as a surprise. He would be dropping by, seemingly spontaneously and unannounced, and the shopkeepers would pretend to be surprised and say how glad they were that he popped in because they had a little gift for him.

The gift was always the same: a bottle of sherry, a Melton Mowbray pork pie, a box of Black Magic chocolates or a bag of mince tarts. These were items agreed upon years ago. The giving and receiving of gifts had evolved into a rite of passage every Christmas. Mr Watson netted quite a haul.

Harold's reputation as a curmudgeon was never in doubt, but at Christmas, something changed, something magical happened, and he was transformed into a more jolly, more chatty, more convivial person.

He puffed more heartily on his pipe, laughed more, talked more, gestured more expressively, and started to punctuate his sentences with a playful stab of his pipe in the air when telling a story.

Somehow, it worked. He made his audience smile. He got them to tell silly stories of their own. In no time at all, he had them all giggling and joking together, grumbling in a good-humoured way about not being paid enough, or recounting crazy antics of customers.

It took Harold a week to visit each and every store. He timed his visits to avoid confusion. He didn't want clients to mix up his Christmas visit with his regular business call.

Every day, he returned to the office with an armful of gifts, some wrapped in tissue paper, some in colourful bags, some open for all to see.

Mrs. Partridge promptly relieved him of his bounty and added it to the growing pile of gifts in the corner. Harold never protested.

The presents were later distributed by Mrs. Partridge, with Harold's consent, first to those of us in the office, then to weekly contributors, such as Sam Small.

Matthew decided it was a good time to sweet-talk Mrs. Partridge into giving him a bottle or something as a Christmas gift to Stan at the café.

"Are you mad?" she protested.

"But Mrs. P, it's Christmas. And Stanley is one of God's children," said Matthew.

"He's a terrible man, Matthew. What are you thinking?" Mrs. Partridge huffed.

"He's our neighbour. We are told to love thy neighbour. Anyway, Stan is really part of our team. He makes great fried egg sandwiches. It lifts our spirits. Well, it always lifts mine," Matthew argued.

"You see something the rest of us don't," said Mrs. Partridge, and Matthew gave her a look of disappointment intended to shame.

"Go on then, take him something," she said. "Do it quickly before I change my mind."

"Thank you, Mrs. P. I will tell him it comes from Miss Marlowe. He'll love that."

Matthew selected a bottle of Harvey's Bristol Cream in a bright red paper bag and also quickly nabbed a box of Black Magic chocolates.

Stan swore at him, as usual, when he walked into the café, but softened when Matthew handed him the gift and told him it was from Miss Marlowe.

"You think this makes up for all the shit you give me all year?" Stan said. 'Merry Christmas, Stanley', said Matthew, stepping out the door.

"What? No egg sandwich today?" Stan called after him.

"Not today, Stanley, but tomorrow and for the rest of my life," Matthew laughed as he closed the door.

* * *

CHAPTER TWENTY
POETRY

I saw the same people every morning when I walked to work. George, the road sweeper, with his brushes and big bin on wheels, was always in the same spot in the market square, outside St. John's.

I had stopped to chat with him once and discovered he had attended art school, gone to Cornwall, and tried to earn a living as an artist.

He knew a lot about art and often attached copies of paintings to his bin to educate the world. He saw it as part of his mission to enlighten others. He told me he was still painting.

"Morning, George," I called to him. "Turner sky today," I said, pointing up at the clouds and the beautiful redness on the horizon. George shook his head and gave me a dismissive, what-do-you-know look, and shouted, "More Monet than Turner. Maybe a little Constable with those clouds."

Arnold the butcher was always outside his shop, vigorously scrubbing the front step and hosing down the pavement. He liked everything spic and span.

No one could get past Arnold without him saying good morning to them and giving a quick weather report. 'Looks like rain," he'd say, or "Going to be lovely all day", or "Whew! It's gonna be a hot one."

Always cheerful and smiling, he was the definition of good-natured. I was always happy to see him. We always spotted each other from a distance. It became a contest to see which of us would say good morning first. He was always delighted when he got the words out first, so I always purposely held back to give him the advantage.

Bath Street was always bustling with life first thing in the morning, with people getting on and off buses, office workers filing into the bank, shopkeepers opening doors, putting out signs and brushing doorways.

The week before Christmas, I caught sight of Dylan Bishop, the teacher from the Steiner school, bobbing along in front of me as he loped down the hill. He was easy to spot, being so much taller than everyone else on the street. His jaunty way of walking made him appear to bob up and down. It was almost as if he were dancing.

I ran to catch up with him, and he greeted me with a big grin, as if I were a relative he hadn't seen in ages. He threw his arms in the air and said, 'Wow, look who it is! Great!' Then, he brought his big hands squarely down on my shoulders and gave me a shake.

"I'm so glad to see you. I have something important to ask you. I hope you won't say no. Will you be part of our poetry reading in St. John's on Sunday night? Going on, say yes."

"Poetry?" I was shocked. Dylan looked up and seemed to go into a trance,

"How clear, how lovely bright.

How beautiful to sight, those beams of morning playing.

How heaven laughs out with glee,

Where, like a bird set free,

Up from the eastern sea,

Soars the delightful day."

As he recited the lines, he used his hands in actions, pretending to hold, then release a bird.

"Yes, poetry. You know poetry. We're all going to read our own poems. It's a Christmas thing. Rev. Alan Rogers has asked us if we would be willing to do it. It'll be fun.

Dylan's bobbed expectantly in front of me, and he beamed with an ear-to-ear grin, his lively, brown eyes twinkling with kindness as he brushed hair from his forehead.

"But I don't write poetry," I said. "I haven't a clue."

"Yes, you do. You can write a poem. You could write something," he said. "It doesn't have to be brilliant or profound or witty or clever, just something light and Christmasy, something fun."

"Others will be there. Mark Bellamy, the English teacher from Blackstone. Jacob Stevens, the ex-mayor. I'm reading, nothing fancy, just scribbling. Come on, you can do it. Your editor will love it."

I was noncommittal. We walked on together. Dylan stopped and put his hand on my shoulder.

"Today I shall be strong,
No more shall yield to wrong,
Shall squander life no more;
Days lost, I know not how,
I shall retrieve them now;
Now I shall keep the vow
I never kept before"

Before I could say a word, Rory Michaels appeared out of nowhere and grabbed me by the arm.

"I need to talk to you," he said.

Dylan waved goodbye and continued bobbing down the hill, turning back to shout, "See you Sunday, St. John's, 6:30, I'll put your name on the program." He was gone before I could protest.

Rory said he had exciting news. The Licensed Victuallers were holding their annual Christmas party on Thursday.

"You have to come. I'm going. It's free food, free drinks. There'll be girls there. It'll be fun."

I said yes. I was thinking about the free food.

"The mayor's Christmas reception is the same night in his parlour. We can go there first, then head to the victuallers' party. What d'you say? It'll be a great night.

"Tell you what. Meet me outside the town hall at 5.30. The mayor's do is at 6, the Victuallers' don't start till 7, so we'll have plenty of time."

He disappeared into the office. I walked on, happy to have friends.

* * *

CHAPTER TWENTY-ONE
JESUS

The Christmas poetry night at St. John's came sooner than I expected. Dylan phoned me at the newspaper to make sure I would be there. He refused to let me off the hook. I told the office. They laughed, especially Dan Wootton.

Since the church was only a short walk from my home, I waited until the very last minute to leave, but I ended up being the first to arrive. I had hoped the event would be cancelled. I thought of leaving. No sooner did the thought cross my mind than Dylan arrived, with his entourage of fellow poets.

The Rev. Rogers followed them into the church and took charge, greeting us and ushering us into the front pews. People began to file in. They were mainly elderly parishioners with not much to do on a Sunday evening.

The Rev. Rogers introduced Dylan and thanked him for agreeing to bring his band of poets together for a Christmas poetry night at the church.

Dylan leapt up and rushed into the pulpit. He was wearing a scarlet shirt, yellow jeans and burgundy shoes. He was the most colourful object in the church, even rivalling the flowers on the altar and the saints in the stained glass windows.

Dylan launched into his poem. It sounded like a pop song.
Laughing, giggling, jumping, dancing
Ever spinning, ever turning.
In the streets, in the windows
Lovers kiss, fire burns.
Christmas comes in many colours
Red and white,
blue and green.
Don't get left always waiting
Always watching,
Always wishing
For what might
have been.

Dylan looked up, flashed a smile and rushed from the pulpit's winding steps.

Mark Bellamy, the English teacher, got up next. He had long, wild Beethoven-like hair and moved furtively as if he knew that one day he would be famous.

In the pew, he had been continually asking those around him if his face was red. They repeatedly told him, "No, it isn't!"

His poems were ponderous and complex, with many obscure references to classical texts and themes. I thought of what a teacher told me about T.S. Eliot at his most inscrutable.

The moment Bellamy began reading, he slipped into a solemn, affected, sonorous tone that made me think of some pitiful, life-weary romantic poets. I didn't understand a word. It all sounded lofty and intellectual, deliberately obscure and monotonous.

Jacob Stevens, the town's former mayor, came next. Stevens had been forced to resign after suffering a nervous breakdown. He spoke with a small, frail, thin voice and read from crumpled sheets of paper, which he held very close to his face.

He described how each day felt like "a wet flannel" being dragged across his face and how nights were long and hard and airless like "the lid snapped tight on a tin of coffee, pressed down hard and sealed so nothing could get in".

He finished with a poem about darkness. He said, "Only sleep sets me free from the ugliness of light", and "Only the silence of night brings me hope of beauty in death."

We were all relieved when he stopped speaking. Stevens returned to the pew, more pale than before, and he slumped down beside me and was trembling.

Dylan's booming baritone voice broke the silence as he introduced me as a "new voice in town". From the pulpit, I stammered about not having done anything like this before. Dylan shot me an impatient look and waved me to get on with it. I said my poem was called *Hippy Christmas*.

Thank you, Jesus
For what you've done
It's Christmas now
And I'm having fun.
All-night party.
Crate of beer.
I'm reading you, Jesus,
Loud and clear.
Thank you, Jesus
For Santa Claus
He's an okay guy
With a switched-on cause.
He stills the blues
He makes us smile
He gives us love,
For a little while
So, thank you, Jesus
For what you've done
It's Christmas now
And I'm having
Fun.

The church was silent like the stillness after a eulogy at a funeral. The Rev. Rogers folded his arms and stared piteously at me, then dropped his eyes to stare at the floor. Dylan leapt up, shook my hand as I returned to my pew.

When it was all over, we all went to the Borough Arms across the street. It turned into a jolly party with everyone talking loudly, laughing, and drinking too much.

Mark Bellamy kept asking people if his face was red. Jacob Stevens kept trying to corner me to talk earnestly about the town council.

"You need to talk to my editor," I said and escaped to talk to Dylan

The evening rolled on. There was laughter, storytelling, a new feeling of camaraderie and a shared sense of purpose. We all agreed to meet again for a poetry night at a pub.

Dylan rushed over when he saw I was leaving. He took my hand, shook it vigorously and said how he hoped we would bump into one another again soon, on the street, outside the school, or at his home for tea and toast.

'You are welcome, anytime," he said. I believed him.

* * *

CHAPTER TWENTY-TWO
PARLOUR

I was on time to meet Rory outside the town hall for the mayor's Christmas party at 6:30 on the dot on Thursday night. It was already dark, and the streets were quiet and deserted.

I wore a suit and tie. Rory came dressed as if he were going to a disco. He was wearing a blue sports coat and a yellow open-neck shirt. His hair was slicked back and shiny. He looked like a rock star.

"Is the Mayor going to like seeing you dressed like that?" I said.

"I don't care," said Rory. "It's a party. It's Christmas."

Rory's plan was to go first to the mayor's Christmas party and then on to the licensed victuallers' Christmas party.

"Two parties in one night! Fantastic," said Rory.

"I have my own invitation to the mayor's do," I said, pulling out the invite from my inside pocket. "It was on my desk this morning."

"Match," said Rory. "I got one, too. Good. So, now we don't have to gate-crash," he laughed. "It would've been okay if we did. They never mind. They know us. They always want us there. But having an official invite is better."

The parlour was already crowded when we arrived. Councillors and council officials were busy rubbing shoulders and trying to cosy up to the town clerk. Everyone had a glass of sherry or beer. There was laughter and the hum of conversation.

One voice boomed louder than the rest. That of the Mayor, His Honour Colin Beatty, who, since it was a formal occasion, was resplendent in his official red gown and weighty gold chain of office.

Behind him, the silver mace was locked in its place of honour, and all around the room were photos in gilt frames of former mayors, all of whom seemed to be smiling and looking directly at me and Rory as if asking, "What the hell are you doing here?"

Rory spotted Maggie Vincent, wearing a stunning red dress, and standing in the middle of the room, surrounded by admirers.

Rory made a beeline for her where she was standing and nudged his way into the circle to get close enough to say hello. I followed in his wake, and we both ended up in the desired, coveted spot, on either side of the beautiful Mrs Vincent.

She recognised Rory. Her face brightened into a relaxed, radiant smile, and her lips parted, revealing her immaculately white teeth. She was a vision of loveliness and perfection that bedazzled us all.

Mrs Vincent touched Rory's arm and continued touching it as she said how nice it was to see him again. Rory blushed with delight and looked over at me to make sure I had witnessed this unexpected gesture of affection. It was something Rory would talk about for the rest of the night.

We didn't get to say anything to Mrs Vincent. She did all the talking. If our attention started to drift, she would touch Rory's arm and quickly change the subject to talk about music, especially her love for classical music.

Nobody cared that she did all the talking. We certainly didn't. We stood silently at her side, like sentries, nodding or laughing at her every word, never interrupting, simply happy to listen and watch her every move.

The mayor's long-suffering, overworked secretary, a short, middle-aged Welsh woman, arrived carrying glasses filled with sherry on a silver tray.

Rory and I each grabbed a glass, took a sip, and grinned at one another, simultaneously thinking what a privilege, what an honour it was to be served in such a grand, formal way, and in the mayor's parlour to boot.

Rory dragged me deeper into the room where there were plates of finger sandwiches, slices of pork pie, cubes of cheese, and piles of sugar-dusted mince pies.

Rory ate quietly and quickly, all the time looking furtively around him to make sure not to be seen to be the happy, indulgent, greedy little badger that he was.

The Rev. Rogers was there. He saw me and frowned. Barry Bushnell and Peter Thompson from the Telegraph turned up.

"You two are having too much fun," said Barry, who looked very dapper in a smartly tailored dark suit and bow tie. Peter shuffled uncomfortably from side to side at Barry's side. He was still in his grey work suit and his crumpled gabardine raincoat.

Rory leaned over and whispered that we should make our departure, but not before shaking the major's hand. We inched our way into line. The mayor was already a little tipsy. His face was red and he was laughing too much. We shook his hand, slipped into the cold marble hallway and out through the heavy wooden main doors into the dark street.

Through the window, we could still see a cluster of admirers trying to help Mrs Vincent on with her coat. She saw us watching her through the window and gave a little wave. We smiled back and walked back. Rory was thrilled

"How old do you think she is?" I asked Rory.

"Some say she's in her 40s. I think she could be in her late 30s. Still very beautiful."

"Does she live in town?" I asked.

"Of course, in a big house on Wellington Crescent. Very fancy," said Rory. "She's rich. Well, her husband's a doctor. We rarely see him. She's always on her own."

"Do you think she's happy?" I said.

"Don't know," said Rory. " But look at her." She was getting into a big black car. "She looks great, doesn't she. I don't see her as sad or lonely. She likes her life, being a councillor and all that. She's on every committee going. Planning. Finance. Library. You name it. And she loves being a magistrate. She doesn't have kids, so I guess this is what she does with her time. It's all a bit of a hobby for her, I reckon."

* * *

CHAPTER TWENTY-THREE
GIN

In the town square, couples holding hands were making their way to the La Scala cinema.

Carollers gathered around the town's Christmas tree. As Rory and I came closer, the carollers began singing Hark the Herald Angels Sing.

Rory pulled me to a standstill to listen. It was a frosty night. We could see the breath of the singers as they sang.

One of the carollers saw us listening and came towards us holding a collection box. Rory dug into his wallet and pulled out a pound note. The choir changed its tune to Joy to the World.

We crossed the square and disappeared down a dark side street on our way to an empty warehouse the Licensed Victuallers had rented for their party.

Inside, we found a bar set up at one end of the room and a row of tables covered by white tablecloths down the middle. Christmas lights were hung everywhere, and a jazz quartet was playing festive tunes.

The bar gleamed and sparkled and was stocked with all the top brands of liquor. I had never seen such a lavish display. Bartenders in white jackets were serving drinks.

"Wow, this is amazing," I said. "I've never been to anything so swish."

"This is just the beginning," said Rory.

Guests were mainly owners of the town's pubs and restaurants, but there were also representatives there from local breweries and companies selling whiskey, gin, and vodka.

We could see a row of kegs of beer hooked up to taps at the bar, more beer than could possibly be drunk in an evening.

"It's a drinker's paradise," said Rory.

At the bar, he insisted that I live a little and try something different.

"Come on, it's all free, remember. No reason to hold back. We're here to have a good time. We deserve it. We work so hard."

He turned to the barman.

"Give him a large G&T," he said. "Same for me."

I had not heard that term before.

"G&T? Gin and tonic," said Rory. "You'll love it. Put a wedge of lemon in mine," he told the barman, looking back at me to see if I appreciated his sophistication. I had no clue.

Rory was only a few years older than me, but this night he thought he needed to take the lead and show me how to have a good time.

"One thing you need to remember about gin," he said. "It's an assassin. You can find your way back from too much wine or beer. Gin is not so forgiving."

"An assassin?" I said.

"When you feel you're going down for the count with whiskey or vodka, wine or beer, there's always a way back," said Rory.

"You can drink water, drink coffee, eat something, wash your face, breathe, go for a walk, jump up and down, do something. You can come back, well, you can get back enough to stand up straight.

"It's not the same with gin. Gin invites you in, seems friendly encugh, but once it gets you in its crosshairs, it takes you out like an assassin. Bang! Out of nowhere. Bam! You're gone. You go down and you don't get up again."

"So your message is . . . don't drink gin?" I shrugged.

"No, what I'm saying is, don't let gin fool you, don't let it put you on your knees. If you let it get the better of you, if you drink too much of it, you're a dead man," said Rory.

The drinks arrived. We clinked glasses without making a toast.

"Isn't this a great atmosphere," he said "Remember, this is one of the perks of the job. Free food, free booze, free entry. We get invited to all the best parties. Good, isn't it. You know you can eat for free all week if you really want to. You just have to crash parties like this. They never mind."

Surveying the room, we noticed waitresses in black dresses carrying food to a long banqueting table. Rory couldn't believe his luck that such a feast was being laid out, not mere snacks, but authentic, solid, hearty dishes: lasagna, meatballs, roast beef, pawns, ham, lamb skewers, roast potatoes, pork chops, plates of cheese, bowls of bread and platters of fruit.

We each grabbed a big plate and joined the lineup, helping ourselves to everything. Rory filled his plate so high that he had a hard time walking back to a table.

The warehouse became more crowded. The band played louder. More drinks were poured. The room got hotter, conversations grew louder, people started laughing, dancing and telling jokes that were best not said in polite company.

It all felt very sophisticated and decadent. It reminded me of a wedding I was once at where after midnight when all the aunts and uncles got drunk and dance wildly together and laugh until they cry and then they started fighting and it all ended in a tears.

Rory insisted on keeping me well supplied with gin and tonics. I never refused. I thought I had developed a taste for gin.

Young, beautiful waitresses were standing together, chatting in a corner on a break. Rory dragged me over to talk to them. He made them laugh, and he wasted no time in telling them that we were reporters working on an important story. Rory did all the talking. He was happy when one of the waitresses gave him her phone number.

The last thing I remember was Rory putting his arm around me as the president of the Licensed Victualers Association told him to make sure I got home safely. How I got home is still a mystery.

I woke up the next morning, still fully dressed, in my bed. Downstairs, I found Rory curled up in a chair, covered up by a skimpy blanket and his sports coat.

I have never drunk gin again. Rory later told me that he was forced to stop twice on the way to my house to allow me to throw up.

"It wasn't a pretty sight," he said. "You were a mess."

"Did anyone see me?" I asked.

"No, thank God. It was late. The streets were empty. Good job, there were no police around. They don't like it when people throw up in the street. It's called drunk and disorderly. You wouldn't want to be up before Mrs. Vincent. And what would Miss Marlowe think?" he said and laughed.

Our friendship was cemented that night. I was always grateful he got me home, but I felt ashamed, but I was more relieved I didn't die in my bed from alcohol poisoning.

* * *

CHAPTER TWENTY-FOUR
ROUNDS

Rory and I parted company outside his office on Friday morning, completing our time together. We said the briefest of goodbyes and agreed to have lunch later at Shepherds.

Gin may be an assassin, but youth was my friend when it came to dealing with my hangover. I was still suffering from guilt and shame when I arrived at the office.

I was not looking forward to having to carry out my list of dreary chores - pinning photographs, wrapping newspapers, fetching coke.

To my relief, Dan Wootton had other plans for me.

"Matthew will do your job today," he announced. "You're coming with me on my rounds. It's what Miss Marlowe wants."

Matthew scowled. I had to conceal my delight, although in that exact moment, I thought about the awkwardness of knowing I would be going somewhere with Dan, who I knew was not my biggest fan.

By "my rounds", he meant delivering free papers to the town hall, post office, library, police station and department store, one of our biggest advertisers.

Each week, he took four papers to each of these places. He

didn't like doing it. It was something Miss Marlowe insisted he do as a gesture of goodwill. She saw it as an opportunity to touch base with important institutions in the community. Dan disagreed. He thought it was a total waste of time.

Before we could leave, Mr Watson came around the corner and handed out pay packets.

"Happy Christmas," he said with a big smile on his face. "Miss Marlowe has put a little gift in there for you all."

It was an extra week's wages. We were all delighted and thanked Harold as if the gift came from him.

Outside, I piled a stack of papers in the boot of Dan's car, and he drove to the top of the town and parked at the market square.

Dan loved his little car. It was a smart, little, blue Ford Anglia, not a very exciting one, but Dan loved it nonetheless.

At the market square, a bus pulled in front of us, forcing him to reverse to make way. From the back seat, I had a clear view out the rear window, and I could see concrete pylons, placed to discourage parking.

"I don't think you should reverse," I said.

Dan ignored me and went backwards very quickly and smashed into the pylons. There was a loud crunching sound.

"What the hell!" yelled Dan.

I said nothing.

He jumped out, looked at the back of his car and saw that the boot was totally smashed and crumpled.

"Did you see that!" Dan yelled at me through the window.

"I told you not to reverse," I said meekly.

"Well, bloody hell! I wish you'd said it louder. Why didn't you yell something?"

He stomped to the rear of the car, and kept swearing, saying "bugger" and "sod it" and "sod it" and "bugger" and then he shot angry look at the bus driver and then an angry look at me, then an angry look at the pylon and then back at me again and said 'bugger' and 'sod it' several more times.

I got out of the car. I was about to say 'Shall I get the papers out of the boot?' but thought better of it.

"Well, you're going to have to deliver these stupid papers on your own," he said. "I've got to get this car fixed. What a bloody mess. Did you see those pylons? Did you?"

I refused to make eye contact.

Dan pried open the lid to the boot and dropped the pile of papers on the ground.

"You take them. Four to the post office, four to the police station, four to the Co-op, the manager's office, four to the library, and four to the clerk's department in the town hall."

He got back into the car and angrily drove away, skidding a little as he accelerated, and the lid of the boot flapped up and down. It was comical, I thought, and I suppressed a smile. The image of a circus clown in a little car came to mind.

Hugging the papers, I surveyed the square and decided to call first at the library, with its beautiful orange brick façade.

Head librarian, Betty Bullock, took the papers from me and guided me into a back room where there was a tray full of mince pies and sugar biscuits.

"Help yourself. Merry Christmas," she said. "It's nice to see a new face."

I hesitated. I didn't feel like drinking again. But Mrs. Bullock insisted I should raise a glass to toast the season. The gathering quickly gained momentum and became more boisterous, with everyone laughing, joking and saying how this was the way we should always work.

It was the same at the post office. The sorting of mail came to a standstill at the insistence of the postmaster, Douglas Bagshot, a big, jovial, welcoming man, surprisingly agile and quick for his size.

The personification of goodwill, Bagshot called all his workers together and told them to help themselves to mince tarts, slices of pork pie, milk chocolates and assorted biscuits in deep tins.

"Don't hold back. You get in there," he said.

He poured me a glass of sherry as I listened to his lament about the ocean of mail that came flooding in day after day.

"It'll keep coming and coming until we shut shop on Christmas Eve," he said. "We never get a break at this time of year. You coming in gives us a reason to take a breather. Thanks for coming."

For a moment, I liked the idea that I was indeed responsible for the festivities. It was, after all, my paper delivery that brought work to a standstill.

"I don't read the Messenger. Never have time. I don't even live in Chesterton. I'm a Derby man myself. I read the Telegraph. But I know Miss Marlowe. She's a gem. A real class act. I like her. That's really why we do this. It was all her idea."

There was no merrymaking at the Co-op. I handed four papers to the store manager's secretary. She smiled and kept on typing. I stood for a moment, wondering if there was a glass of sherry or a mince pie. She looked up at me and stared sternly until I left.

At the police station, I expected law and order as usual. There was a small, oblong window at the front counter through which the duty officer always bent down awkwardly to speak to reporters. He stayed on his side, we stayed on ours.

Christmas was different. This time, there was a change in procedure. The counter door was swung open, and I was invited into the inner sanctum of the operations room.

Constables, in their smart, buttoned-down uniforms, acted differently. They were smiling and cracking jokes. Instead of stern, sombre and serious, they were friendly, outgoing and good-humoured,

Inside the operations room, I was treated to a rare view of the operations hub where the helmets and truncheons were kept and a quick look into the cells.

There was a Christmas tree, decorated with tinsel and lights.

The chief inspector offered me a tray of mince pies, chocolates, and biscuits.

"You're not stealing," he winked. "It's no crime to treat yourself at Christmas." I did.

My last stop was the clerk's office at the town hall.

"We saw you last night," said the receptionist with the Welsh accent. "At the mayor's do. Did you have a good time?"

Before I could answer, she answered for me.

"Looks like you did. And that other fellow, the one who was with you, he didn't hold back, did he? Mind you, it was good, wasn't it?"

I placed the last four papers on the counter. Then, I remember that the receptionist was the same woman in the black trouser suit who had been serving the glasses of sherry.

She pointed me to a small plate of biscuits and a thin splattering of chocolates. It was a relatively meagre offering, even miserly, I thought, compared to what I had been offered at the library, post office and police station.

"That's all we've got for you today," she said with a feigned look of disappointment. "But you did well last night, didn't you. We should all be so lucky."

I smiled, said Merry Christmas, and left. Outside the town hall, the clock on St. John's tower struck noon. The carollers were back under the big Christmas tree. They started singing Away in a Manger.

If I ran down Bath Street and made it just in time, as Rory was going into the Shepherds for lunch. He smiled, happy to see me, and stepped aside to allow me to go ahead of him.

It started snowing. It was Christmas Eve.

* * *

CHAPTER TWENTY-FIVE
JANUARY

Androcles was dancing with the lion. It was the second week in January, 1969, and I was in the audience at Chesterton Grammar school watching a production of Androcles and the Lion, a play by George Bernard Shaw.

I was there to review the play for the paper, but Dan had been told me not to be overly critical, not to expect professional standards.

Instead, he said I should concentrate on writing down as many names as possible: names of cast members, names of the kids doing the costumes, lighting and the scenery.

The drama teacher, Miles Rathbone, tall and slim with uncombed hair and a theatrical way of speaking. came to where I was sitting.

"We're delighted you could come," he said, putting his arm around me as I sat in my seat. "I love the way the scenery turned out. We spent a lot of time doing research, looking at photos of Rome, to get it right.

"Anyway, good of you to come. Enjoy the play. See you later," he said and dashed away.

It took me back to my own school days and a particular moment when I asked a teacher about Greek myths.

"Don't worry about that, it's never going to concern you," the teacher told me.

How different, I thought, Rathbone was being, so keen to communicate and give his students such creative, enriching learning experiences. For a moment, I wish I could have gone to this school and had Rathbone for my teacher.

Watching Androcles dance with the lion made me realise all that I'd been missing. I was not angry, bitter or resentful, but grateful and glad to be a reporter assigned to watch such a wonderful play.

The story of Androcles touched me deeply. I was gripped by the fable of the slave who removed a thorn from a lion's paw and was later rewarded for his act of kindness when the lion recognised him and refused to savage him in the arena.

I understood instinctively the truth of the story that an unconscious, selfless act of kindness could indeed come back unexpectedly in the form of a reward.

As I watched Androcles dancing with the lion, I thought back to my wild run down Bath Street to get to my interview at the Messenger on time, and how I had been rewarded by Miss Marlowe. It all made perfect sense.

I was not the only one laughing at Androcles dancing with the lion. We were all laughing. It was joyous.

* * *

There was nothing to laugh about in the council chamber at the town hall. Ron Wilson was in the Press gallery, busily taking notes at a tense and sombre meeting of the finance committee.

Councillor Maggie Vincent was arguing for an increase in funding for her pet project, the improvement of the gardens in the Victoria Arboretum, Chesterton's central park.

She was being opposed by the mayor, Colin Beatty, who insisted there was no money for such a frivolous expenditure.

"We don't have money for pansies and petunias, daffodils

and dahlias," he bellowed, pleased with his unusually poetic turn of phrase. "We can't be penny-wise and pound-foolish. We have bigger fish to fry."

"We need beautiful parks and gardens," said Councillor Vincent. "Beauty is what binds us together. Parents need beautiful places to take their children.

"This is not frivolous spending. It is an investment in community health and well-being," she added, and other councillors applauded.

Ron kept scribbling away, desperate to write down every word. Barry, with the Telegraph, and Rory, with the Post, were also there, frantically taking copious notes.

Barry was unfazed and completely relaxed. His 200-words-a-minute shorthand was more than adequate to deal with the rapid exchanges.

A vote was called. There was a show of hands. Councillor Vincent won by two votes. She smiled triumphantly and looked over at the Press table to make sure everyone was paying attention to her victory.

The mayor grunted and groaned, shook the papers in front of him, and stroked them flat, pressing down on them with his large, tubby hands.

"Next issue, revenues!" he announced grumpily. "And I believe you will very quickly see that our expenditures already far exceed our income. I hope you all give that some thought!

He shot a stern look at the Press gallery. Rory grinned, which made the mayor even more grumpy.

* * *

Out in the country, at Cossall parish council, Matthew White was falling asleep in his chair.

He had been listening for more than an hour to villagers discussing the need to keep footpaths open as a right of way across farmers' fields.

Before this, they had also talked for an hour about the need to restore the village's medieval stone well.

Matthew's eyes kept closing involuntarily. He tried propping up his head with his hand, but this caused him to fall asleep and almost bang his head on the desk.

At long last, Matthew thought it was over, but then someone asked about who was looking after twitchels and stiles. Matthew groaned loud enough for the whole room to hear.

The discussion about footpaths had been agonising enough, but the topic of twitchels was unbearable. Matthew could barely conceal his disdain and discomfort.

The parish councillors were oblivious to Matthew's groans. They loved their village, loved talking about village issues, loved being together at the meetings. It was all painfully dull and mundane to Matthew. It was a fun night out for the parish council in Cossall.

* * *

In her cosy cottage, not far from the Hemlock Stone, Mrs Partridge sat beside her husband in their matching chintz armchairs in front of the fire. Mrs Partridge was reading an Agatha Christie mystery. Mr Partridge was reading about European pilgrimages.

They were comfortable and content in their silence, rarely saying a word to one another, perfectly happy to sit together, reading, and listening to the sound of the coal fire as it glowed and crumbled and radiated warmth and light across the room.

* * *

Dan Wootton was busily rattling away at his typewriter in the basement of his home, composing a letter of application for the job as editor of a weekly paper in the seaside town of Eastbourne.

Dan was tired of Chesterton. He was weary of the bleakness, the poverty, the grittiness and grimness of the place, and he longed for a new life in the sunshine, in the land of pebbly beaches, breezes and bandstands, promenades and piers, and the smell of the sea.

He paused from his rat-a-tat-tapping and looked more closely at the words on the white sheet of paper.

Then, he snatched the paper from the roller, crumpled it and squeezed it into the size and shape of a snowball, and slammed it with some force into the waste basket.

He was determined to get this application right. He had to get it right. He needed the new job desperately.

He could already see himself walking beside the sea in his open-neck shirt and summer slacks and beach shoes.

He smiled as if he could already feel the sun on his face.

* * *

In Cotmanhay, one of Chesterton's working-class neighbourhoods, Harold Watson was in the kitchen with his wife Mildred.

Harold was smoking his pipe as he pored over a garden catalogue and tried to decide which vegetable seeds to order.

Mildred was slicing up beetroot for Harold's sandwich. She paused occasionally to wipe her hands and go over and see whatever it was Harold wanted her to see in his catalogue.

Mildred didn't mind the pipe smoke. She didn't mind making Harold's sandwiches. It was all part of their life together.

She put on the kettle. Harold put his catalogue down and turned on the radio.

They sat across the kitchen table from one another, sipping their tea as they listened to a programme about big band music in the 1940s.

Harold reached for the catalogue, flipped it open and pointed at pictures of tomatoes and onions. Mildred nodded and smiled approvingly.

They drank their tea and listened to the Tommy Dorsey band playing Marie.

* * *

Brenda lived with her mother, Pat, now a widow.

Every Tuesday night, Brenda's cousins, Sophie and Maureen, came round to play cards. They always sat at the kitchen table, drank pop, ate cake, and talked about work, TV shows, and any gossip they'd heard.

Brenda was the life and soul of the party. She laughed easily and spoke the loudest. She was always the one to tell the most outrageous stories.

She was also quick to compliment her cousins on their intelligent choices in clothes and hairstyle. Brenda's mom said little, but sat and smiled and was happy for the company.

They all loved one another. It was obvious the moment the cousins walked in. It was evident in the way Brenda took their coats, embraced them, and brought them into the kitchen.

No one could remember how the weekly get-together got started. It had been going for years. It was something they all loved dearly.

When it was time to say good night, there were sighs, hugs, kisses and sweet words about taking care and staying safe. Goodbyes were always long and drawn out.

* * *

Miss Marlowe was tucked up in her large, canopied four-poster bed, fragrant white sheets billowing around her and big, soft, plump pillows under her head.

She was reading her favourite book, What It's Like to Die, a compilation of accounts by people who had been certified dead, either on an operating table or at the scene of an accident, and had miraculously recovered and returned to life with stories of what they had seen and experienced on the Other Side.

Miss Marlowe was a sceptic, but she was intrigued by the obvious sincerity and conviction of the storytellers. She was trying to decide whether they were telling the truth, or if they had been sorely misled by their senses, or if they were just simply charlatans and tricksters out to swindle and take advantage of the gullible.

She read a few more pages, then closed the book, took off her glasses, placed them on the night table, switched off the lamp and sank back into her stack of pillows with a sigh.

She preferred to sleep in an upright, sitting position. It was something she had always done all her life on the advice of her father, who believed too many people die in their sleep because they were lying flat on their backs.

In the corner of her bedroom, there was a small fireplace, a simple, black iron grate, but perfectly capable of lifting the chill from the room, filling it with a warm light.

Miss Marlowe's breathing grew softer and quieter as she gently drifted off to sleep, the light from the fire still flickering across the room.

* * *

CHAPTER TWENTY-SIX
TRAGEDY

At Stapleton Ironworks, alarms were blaring, sirens were wailing, and emergency lights were flashing. Panic and chaos filled the air.

Workers were running and shouting, calling out for help, distraught and desperate for someone to do something.

A mighty Sentinel locomotive, shunting enormous hoppers of molten metal, had collided with stationary freight cars.

The hoppers had jumped the track, overturned with a thunderous crash, spilling a river of molten metal over the tracks.

Four men had been walking alongside the train. They were engulfed instantly in the lethal flood of liquid fire, as deadly and unstoppable as lava from a volcano.

The men had died instantly, their bodies dissolved by the molten metal in seconds. Eye-witnesses knew the men and were able to give their names to emergency crews at the scene.

A few workers had escaped with minor injuries, cuts, burns and bruises, caused by flying metal shards from the overturned hoppers and crumpled rolling stock.

The noise of the crash had been deafening. Initially, it had been dismissed as just another sudden, nerve-jarring sound from the foundry. But those in the know knew the noise was inconsistent with the usual sounds of routine thuds and bangs coming from ironworks.

It was common for workers to say that they never got used to the unexpected banging and slamming of heavy objects being dropped or bumped.

They said it "creeped" them out, but they accepted that they had to live with it as the price they paid to earn a living. They regarded it as a shared fearfulness that brought them closer together.

They learned to laugh about their harsh working conditions, but they said they could never relax, not for a minute, because all around them, all the time, were the sights and sounds of life-threatening danger and potential disaster.

But on this rainy Tuesday night in January, the blaring sirens, flashing lights and buzzing alarms were something entirely new. Everyone knew immediately that something terrible had happened.

Men had come running from all directions, out of workshops, sheds, across rail lines and along rough gravel paths. They were stopped in their tracks when they arrived at the accident scene with orange fumes rising from the molten metal spill. Some stood open-mouthed in disbelief. Others put their hands over their faces and turned away. Some cried.

CHAPTER TWENTY-SEVEN
DETAILS

The next morning, Dan Wootton assigned us all to cover the story and gather as much information as possible.

"We need all the detail we can get," he said. "We need the names of those who died. We need as much background on them as possible. Readers will want to know who they were and where they lived."

Matthew was sent to the hospital to check on the injured. Ron and I were sent to Stapleton to talk to Alistair Middleton, the ironworks' Press officer.

It was raining when we arrived at the gates of the foundry. We huddled under umbrellas. Through the gates, we could see the toppled locomotive and hoppers. Lights on the top of emergency vehicles were still flashing in the distance. Floodlights illuminated the area. A blanket of grey, brooding cloud darkened the skies overhead.

Alistair Middleton, a kind, well-spoken, educated man in his 50s, was someone Ron liked and respected. Ron called him "a gentleman with a good heart."

Alistair met us at the gate. His face was ashen, and he spoke quietly and softly, acutely conscious of the need to communicate respectfully and sensitively.

"We can't go any farther. This is as close as I can get you to the accident site," said Alistair. "We'll be looking into all this for weeks to come, but I do have some details for you."

Holding a black umbrella over his head, he read from a clipboard.

"Four men have died," he confirmed. "A train collided with parked containers and jumped the tracks. The train was pulling four hoppers of molten metal. When it left the tracks, the train pulled the hoppers with it, causing the hot slag to spill."

He paused, tightened his lips, finding it hard to speak.

"No trace of the men was found, only teeth. We have identified the dead from eyewitnesses who saw them before the crash."

The thought of only teeth being found shocked us all into silence. The image was horrifying.

"All the men were local," Alistair continued. "They lived here in the village," he said, nodding in the direction of Stapleton-by-Dale.

"They had worked for us for years. Two of them were related, father and son, John Abbott and his son Peter. The other two were David Mason and Keith Dawes, both young, married men with kids.

"John Abbott was in his 60s and was close to retirement. His son Peter was in his 30s and worked in the offices. He was well known to everyone here. I often saw him waiting at the gates to walk home with his dad."

"David and Keith worked on the train. They were taking molten metal and slag from the furnaces when the accident happened. They are thought to have jumped from the train when it left the track, but they didn't escape the spill."

Alistair stopped and composed himself. He looked as if it was physically painful to speak. He was determined not to talk in any way that might come across as casual or matter-of-fact.

"This has been an appalling loss of life. It is a tragedy and has devastated the whole community."

We all stood for a moment in silence, the rain hitting our umbrellas and our breath turning to vapour in the cold, damp air.

Ron asked for more details about the cause of the accident.

Alistair shook his head and declined to give more information.

"Everything is under investigation. It would be wrong for me to speculate. I know nothing more. There will be an inquiry. An inquest has already been arranged.

"This is the worst accident in our history. We've seen crushed hands, broken toes, bad burns, and lost fingers, but nothing like this. We're all in shock. Of course, we want to make sure nothing like this ever happens again."

From the ironworks, Ron and I went into the village. Ron talked to people in the street as well as those in the village shop and local pub. I knocked on doors and spoke with the vicar at the church.

Everything people told me, I wrote down. They all said the same thing: how sad it all was, what a tragedy, how they couldn't stop crying. One person told me how he often saw Peter Abbott riding his bike home for lunch.

The vicar said he knew all the men. He had married David Mason only a couple of months ago. The vicar said he had already been in touch with all the families and was arranging a funeral service.

Slowly, we gathered more and more details about the men and their lives. Peter Abbott played for the village cricket team, and Keith Dawes liked football and was a regular at The Stanhope Arms. I learned John Abbott was on the parish council and was getting ready to retire and wanted to go travelling.

I had never done anything like this before, going around gathering information about people who had died in a tragic accident. It felt macabre and intrusive. What right did I have to ask such personal, sensitive questions about people I had never met?

Ron reminded me that we needed to tell the men's story because people wanted to see them remembered, and it was how we showed that they were valuable members of the community.

I went from cottage to cottage, asking people for their thoughts, feelings and remembrances. Slowly, bit by bit, I filled my notebooks.

Dan devoted the front page and two inside pages to the tragedy. The headline, in giant letters, said, STAPLETON TRAGEDY. Under the headline were the words, Ironworks and village mourn four killed in horrific accident.

We ran photos of the men. Matthew got stories from the hospital about people who had a narrow escape. Ron and I told stories about the men who died.

Tears filled my eyes as I typed. I imagined tears were in readers' eyes when they read the stories.

CHAPTER TWENTY-EIGHT
INQUESTS

February was even bleaker than January in Chesterton. There seemed to be less, not more, light, and it never stopped raining.

Even with a cosy, toasty fire, it was bleak and dark and depressing in my little terraced house. I struggled to keep my spirits up.

The tragedy of the Stapleton disaster still weighed heavily on my mind. It was probably the worst possible time to be sent to cover my first inquest.

Why newspapers were allowed to cover inquests was a mystery to me. Why we were permitted to write down such intimate details, particularly when the inquest was into a case of suicide, never seemed right. It felt like a gross invasion of privacy: insensitive, crude and vulgar. But reporting was allowed and it was something I was ordered to do.

Why readers needed to know why a person had ended their life, and details of the method they chose to do it, was always complete baffling to me. But newspapers in 1960s were allowed to report details, regardless of how gruesome or upsetting they were.

Dan Wootton expected me to get every crumb of information, leaving nothing out, and I had to tell the story as if it were a Shakespearean tragedy. It never felt right.

My first inquest involved the awful death of Jonathan Wilkins, a 12-year-old boy who had accidentally drowned in the canal.

"Afternoon, gentlemen," said Dr. Womersley, the town coroner, as he swept into his office and dropped files and photographs of the incident on the desk.

Rory, from the Post, and Peter, from the Telegraph, were already in their seats. I was the last to arrive. Dr. Womersley wasted no time giving details.

"Police were called to the banks of the canal at 4 p.m. on February 10, after Jonathan Wilkins, 12, of 92 Walker Street, was found floating, lifeless in the water.

"What appears to have happened is that Jonathan was riding his bike along the towpath when the cuff of his trouser leg got caught in the chain.

"Jonathan lost his balance and fell from the towpath into the canal. His leg was snagged in the chain, and he despite his best efforts, he was unable to break free."

At this point, Dr. Womersley handed around black-and-white photographs. One showed the boy, facedown in the water, with the bicycle stuck in the mud beneath him.

"Police pulled Jonathan's body from the canal and I was able to conduct an examination," said Dr. Womersley.

"It was my opinion then - and the opinion of the police officers present - that the boy had tried to fight his way free.

"Sadly, he was unable to free himself. Instead, it appears the weight of the bicycle pulled him down deeper into the water. The bike acted like an anchor and became fixed in the mud.

"There were cuts on his hands from Jonathan grabbing the bicycle chain and bruises consistent with his arms hitting the sharp edges of the metal pedals.

"He was clearly in a terrible panic. Struggling may have made things worse. It is conceivable that he might have been able to get out of his trousers and reach the surface for air. Sadly, that's not what happened. I doubt anyone could hold their breath that long. It all happened so fast. I doubt he had much of a chance.

"Unfortunately, there was no one else on the towpath at the time to come to his aid. He drowned in relatively shallow water, eight or 10 feet at most."

The only sound in the coroner's office was the scribbling of ballpoint pens and the rustle of notebook pages being flipped over.

"There's a sad irony to this tragedy," said Dr. Womersley. "Jonathan was on his way to do his brother's paper route.

"His brother, two years older, apparently was unable to do his paper round that day, so Jonathan had offered to do it for him.

"But Jonathan was late and was rushing to get to the newsagent's shop when the accident occurred."

Dr. Womersley looked at us, trying to decide whether to say what he was thinking.

"How do I say this. The family is naturally in shock. They couldn't bear to be here today. It was too painful. The older brother is devastated. Understandably. I wonder if It would be better to leave out the information about Jonathan going to do his brother's paper route."

Dr. Womersley scrutinised our faces, trying to gauge our reaction, then he re-shuffling papers on his desk and resumed his summation.

"I'm going to record a verdict of death by misadventure. This was most definitely a tragic accident. No question. But, sad to say, Jonathan was riding fast along the towpath, a route he was not familiar with. He was riding along a narrow path beside the canal. It is a small space.

"There is no suggestion of negligence or unnecessary risk-taking, but it is also clear there was always the risk that something like this could happen, especially when you're doing an activity that requires balance and your full attention next to a body of water."

With the verdict recorded, the inquest was over. Dr. Womersley invited us up to his desk to see more photos.

One loomed out at me. It was the face of Jonathan, after he had been lifted from the canal and his body laid out, face up, on the grass verge.

His face was white and lifeless, without expression, with no sign of pain or trauma, no blood or bruising. His skin was ghostly white and his hair was wet and tangled. It could have been the face of a boy who had just run out of the pool at the local lido and was resting on his towel in the sun.

Outside the coroner's office, Rory and Peter discussed what Womersley had said about not mentioning the angle of the paper route.

"It's not my job to leave out facts," said Peter indignantly. "That's for my editors to decide."

Rory nodded in agreement.

"The problem is, it's ironic. The boy wouldn't have been there, he wouldn't have been riding along the towpath, but for his decision to help his brother," said Rory.

"I'm leaving it in. In fact, I'll probably lead with it. 'Boy who tried to help his brother by doing his paper route ended up losing his life.'"

Peter agreed. They looked at me, although neither of them really cared what I thought. They were wondering what I intended to do.

"What about the fact that the coroner asked us not to use it?" I said. "Should we put that in?"

"Definitely not." said Rory and Peter in unison.

They reasoned that Dr. Womersley was a thoroughly decent man who was trying to spare the family further pain and upset, not trying stop us doing our job.

"He's not a reporter," said Rory. "He doesn't see how much stronger the story is with this detail in it. Anyway, it's more likely to evoke sympathy and support for the family. The kid died trying to help his brother."

"Okay, it's settled," said Peter. "We're all using it."

We did.

* * *

CHAPTER TWENTY-NINE
SUICIDE

Suicides were a fairly common occurrence in Chesterton. Depression, especially among coal miners and ironworkers, was a darkness that drove many to lose their enthusiasm for life.

The bleakness of winter, dreariness of life down the pit, harshness of work at the ironworks with its grim landscape and punishing daily grind, were key factors that drove more than a few tired and weary souls to drink and despair and ultimately to the grim decision to take their own life.

The English, some say, have only two choices - to laugh or to cut their throat. It was a sad fact that many despairing souls, especially in the unshakable darkness of a cold Derbyshire winter, found themselves in a world drained of interest and empty of joy or hope.

Who knows why, but in the bleakest month of winter, I found myself being assigned to more and more inquests.

It was so cold those days, Rory and I didn't even bother to take off our overcoats. We wore scarves and gloves, and we only removed our gloves when we needed to take notes.

Dr. Womersley, the town coroner, was particularly grim-faced when he knew he was dealing with a suicide.

It was dark outside when Rory and I arrived at his office. The wintry street were dark and empty, but it felt even darker and gloomier inside Womersley's office

Rory and I listened sombrely as the coroner told us about the latest case, the story of an elderly man, close to retirement, who had come home from work to find that his wife of 40 years had hanged herself from a beam at the top of the stairs.

The shock of seeing her limp, lifeless body was so devastating that he had collapsed and fractured his skull on the stone floor.

He might have died but for the fact that the next-door neighbour came running to investigate the reason for the noise when she heard him cry out and fall.

Dr. Womersley said the woman had been taking tranquillisers for a nervous condition. She had been struggling with feelings of sadness over the sudden death of her mother.

"It was all too much," said Dr. Womersley. "She just could not cope with it The writing was on the walls for weeks."

A week later, I was back in the coroner's office to cover the inquest of an elderly farmer who had left his house early one morning and gone into the yard where there was a stone trough for dipping sheep.

Dr. Womersley explained how the farmer had carefully removed the heavy lid of the trough and then deliberately forced his head into the black water and sludge.

"It's hard to imagine the effort this took," said Dr. Womersley. "I'm aghast by the sheer physical strength it took to lift the stone lid. And I cannot begin to imagine the sadness that would drive a man to hold himself under water until he was dead."

Womersley always concluded suicide inquests with the exact same words: "The deceased took his/her life while the balance of their mind was disturbed."

It was the received wisdom of the day that no one in their right mind would ever want to end their life. If they did, regardless of the pain, suffering or anxiety they were experiencing, it must surely be a flaw in their thinking, a mark of a mind broken, troubled, unhinged and disturbed.

Of all the assignments I was given as a junior reporter, the job of reporting a suicide inquest was the absolute worst and most upsetting. It was hard to sleep at night after hearing details of a suicide.

At the Messenger, Brenda and Mrs. Partridge were the office's buoyant optimists, the corks of cheerfulness, never overwhelmed by crashing waves of despair or desperation.

They were always chatty and jubilant, the hub of unsinkable positivity, the reason office morale was always upbeat, lively and good-humoured.

Mrs. Partridge insisted on telling us about how beautiful the sunrise had been that morning, or how thoughtful someone had been on the bus to work, or how kind Miss Marlowe had been.

Brenda never missed an opportunity to buy fresh flowers to brighten up the office, and she often brought in fresh-baked biscuits and slices of cake, and was always quick to share a box of chocolates.

"Better to light one small candle than to curse the dark," she would say as she placed new flowers in the little vase on her counter.

If she noticed any of us dragging our feet, or with an unhappy look on our face, she would stop us and say, "Hey, it may never happen," and she would follow this up with a smile and the offer of a piece of chocolate.

"Go on," she would say, "Treat yourself. You deserve it. You've been working so hard." We always laughed and did as we were told.

Mrs. Partridge took a different approach, very English and sensible. If she thought the office had lost its bounce and was sinking into a malaise of grumpiness or lost in a cloud of melancholia, she would proclaim, very loudly: "Okay, time for tea! Yes, I know we've already had one today, but it's time for another. Everyone, stop what you are doing and come for a cuppa. And there's an extra dipping biscuit for anyone who wants one."

Surprisingly, it worked. It did the trick. Immediately, the spell would be broken, the gloom lifted, the darkness vanquished, and we would all start to talk and laugh.

Tea and sympathy. The cup that cheers. It's the English way.

CHAPTER THIRTY
GOODBYE

Dan Wootton got a swift response from the Gazette in Eastbourne to his job application.

A letter arrived at his home by return mail asking him to come for an interview, which he did, without saying a word to anyone in the office.

He booked a few days off, telling everyone he and his wife were going away for a little holiday.

When he returned, he was in such a jolly, buoyant mood that we all wondered if he had come into money. He was certainly not his usual grump self.

None of us knew the reason for his sudden cheerfulness. Neither did Miss Marlowe. But she was soon to find out.

Dan wasted no time in asking to see her in her study, where he started by talking about how happy he had been at the Messenger, and what a journey of discovery it had been for him, both in terms of his professional development and also his personal growth and experience.

Miss Marlowe quickly tired of this preamble and raised her eyebrows and sighed wearily. She was a wise woman, a keen judge of character, and had a pretty good idea of what was coming.

The more Dan went on about how grateful he was for his time at the Messenger, the more she knew she was about to hand in his resignation.

Finally, when Dan got to the point and said he got a job as editor of a newspaper in Eastbourne, Miss Marlowe gave a deep sigh of relief that he had stopped waffling, although she was somewhat disappointed that it was the first she had heard about his desire to move on. Now, Dan felt free to show his true emotions, his genuine excitement about his new job.

"We're thrilled," he said. "My wife loves Eastbourne. We both do. She's packing as we speak. We've been there a few times for holidays and always loved it."

Miss Marlowe smiled, allowed him to exhale, and compose himself. She did not interrupt or show any impatience. When the opportunity came for her to speak, she wished Dan success and happiness.

"When do you plan to leave?" she asked.

"As soon as possible," said Dan. "I thought by the end of the month. I told the owners of the paper I could give two weeks' notice."

"Two weeks is a short time indeed," said Miss Marlowe with a slight groan. "Editors are not easy to find. Good editors, even harder. But we'll manage, don't you fret. You get off to Eastbourne. Sounds like the land of milk and honey. I hope you and Mrs Wootton will be very happy there. "

Dan got up and was about to leave.

"How do you want to tell the staff?" asked Miss Marlowe.

"Oh, I think you should tell them," said Dan. "I'm not good at goodbyes. I don't think it should come from me."

"As you like," said Miss Marlowe.

The moment he was gone, she picked up the phone and asked Mr Watson to come and see her.

Harold was flabbergasted when she told him the news.

"Well, I never!" he said. "He's a bit of a dark horse, isn't he. He never said a word. I knew nothing about it. When did he go to Eastbourne? It must have been when he took that week off. Well, I'm shocked. I thought the least he would have done is tell me, give me the heads up."

"Yes, yes, Harold, that's all well and good, but what are we going to do now. We can't sit about twiddling our thumbs. He'll be gone in a couple of weeks, and we need to carry on. We don't have much time."

Harold thought for a moment, then his face quickly brightened.

"What about Ron?" he said.

Miss Marlowe said nothing. She was pondering the idea. She walked to her armchair by the fireplace, and Harold followed.

"He can do the work. He knows the town. He's a local boy. He's been doing great work for the past year. I think he could handle it. I think he would do a great job."

"Let me think about it. I'm not saying yes, I'm not saying no," said Miss Marlowe. "It's a big decision. Say nothing to Ron right now. And not a word to Dan, not that he would care. I don't want him to know what we are thinking right now."

Miss Marlowe told Harold to say nothing to the rest of us, not until a new editor had been found.

"We will make both announcements at the same time, the fact that Dan is leaving and the name of the new editor," she said.

"For the moment, say nothing, not even to Jane Partridge. I know how much you like her. I know how close you two are. But I want to keep this between us for the time being."

The following Friday, I was busy doing my chores - pinning photos in the window, wrapping newspapers for dispatch - when Mr Watson came and whispered in Ron's ear. Ron immediately got up and went into the back room to see Miss Marlowe.

This was unusual. Mrs. Partridge and Brenda noticed immediately that something was going on. We all looked at one another, perplexed and curious.

"Is Ron in trouble?" I said.

"No, can't be," said Brenda. "What do you think?" she mused, looking to Mrs. Partridge for her expert opinion.

"I've no idea," she said. "I doubt it's anything important, or I would know. I always know."

"You don't know everything," said Matthew, cheekily with a wicked twinkle in his eye.

Harold and Ron returned. Harold called us to gather next to the stove.

"Okay, I have an important announcement," he began. "First, Dan is leaving. He has got a new job in Eastbourne. He's technically already gone. He won't be back in the office.

"Second, I'm very pleased to announce that Ron will be taking over as editor. Okay, there you have it. Back to work."

Harold put his pipe back in his mouth, took a couple of puffs, and looked over the top of his glasses to see how we had received the news.

I was the first to shake Ron's hand. I congratulated him, and I did it without a trace of insincerity. Brenda was excited, she gave Ron a hug. Matthew said 'well done' rather weakly and unenthusiastically and went back to typing at his desk.

Mrs. Partridge's feathers were ruffled. She had conflicting emotions. She was pleased for Ron, but she was miffed that she had been kept in the dark and not been consulted. She had questions. Why was Dan leaving? Why did Harold keep it secret?

She shot Harold a penetrating look, but he dodged it, puffed on his pipe, and looked away, deliberately avoiding eye contact. Ron was left answering all questions.

"Dan is going to the Eastbourne Gazette, that's all I know. He wants to live by the sea. He apparently loves Eastbourne," he told us.

"He didn't tell me anything. I only found out about all of this a few minutes ago. It's all still a shock to me, too."

"A good shock," said Brenda. "You're going to be the boss.

Fantastic. You deserve it. Well done." And she gave Ron another hug.

It was true. Ron did deserve it. He was a first-rate reporter, and we all felt confident he would be a terrific editor. Secretly, I was delighted that Dan was leaving. I never thought he liked me, and I knew he never wanted to hire me in the first place. I was glad he was gone.

When everything quietened down, Mrs Partridge crept up behind Harold, put her hands on his shoulder and said, "I need to speak to you in private."

Harold didn't move.

"Not right now," he said. "I have pay packets to get out."

It was a snub that Mrs. Partridge would not forget. It was a turning point in their relationship. From that moment, she was less friendly, even frosty, to Harold, who surprisingly didn't seem to care.

It was as if Dan's leaving, Ron's promotion and his deepened relationship with Miss Marlowe as trusted confidante had somehow elevated Harold to a new sense of authority and prestige. All this set him free from Mrs. Partridge's perpetual scrutiny, evaluation and cajoling. He was a much happier man from that moment on.

Dan left without fanfare. No farewell party. No speech.

In Eastbourne, he walked the windy promenade with his wife. He smiled and looked out at the sea. Waves were crashing on the shore. He held tightly on to the new hat he was wearing, just in case the wind snatched it from his head and sent it spinning down the beach.

A few weeks after Dan left, Matthew announced that he, too, would be going. He had been hired as chief reporter with a bigger weekly newspaper in Mansfield.

"It's my hometown," he told us as we gathered around the stove at tea time. "My parents are delighted that I will be so close to home." He lifted his eyebrows and gave a pained look, but then smiled to show he was only joking.

"Whatever will Stan do without you?" I joked.

"You'll have to buy more fried egg sandwiches," said Matthew. "You don't want to make him angry. Who knows what he might say."

We laughed and continued enjoying our tea.

Mr. Watson didn't even leave his chair. He didn't have time for small talk anymore. Mrs. Partridge looked over at him and sighed.

It was yet another loss.

* * *

CHAPTER THIRTY-ONE
COMEUPPANCE

Miss Marlowe had not been seen for weeks after Dan left for Eastbourne, and Ron had assumed his new role as editor of the Messenger.

We all thought she was busy with family matters. The truth was she had been sick, and at one point, had become so ill that she was rushed to the hospital in the middle of the night.

I didn't know she had been unwell until the day she asked me to come and see her in her parlour.

When I opened the door and stepped into the dimly lit room, I could see her slumped in her favourite armchair in front of the coal fire she never allowed to go out.

"Come in, come over here, sit with me by the fire," she said. "I have something I need to talk to you about."

I slipped into the chair beside her. It was the first time I'd seen her in months, but I could see immediately that she was unwell.

Her skin was grey, her eyes were dark and sunken, and her hair was thin and uncombed. It was the most dishevelled I had ever seen her.

"How long have you been with us now? What is it? Almost a

year?" she began. "I've been keeping an eye on you. Did you know that?"

I shook my head. I had no idea. I didn't think she was that interested in what I did.

"Well, I have been keeping an eye on you. And I've been asking others about you. I always want to know how you're doing, if you're learning what you need to learn, if you're becoming the reporter I want you to be, the journalist I believe you can be."

She paused, coughed, took out a handkerchief, wiped her lips, then took a sip of water from a glass.

"What I need to tell you, Steven (she smiled when she spoke my name as if it were a private joke between us), what I need you to understand is that we have some concerns."

"Concerns? Oh dear, that doesn't sound good," I said, alarmed bells going off in my head as I sat more erect and alert.

"Yes, well, I've heard that you enjoy being a reporter very much. In fact, you enjoy the life of a reporter far more than you like doing the job of a reporter."

"I don't understand," I said.

"Well, reporters have a fun life, you know. They get to go to a lot of functions. Parties, receptions, previews, that sort of thing. It's all fuss and nonsense as far as I'm concerned, but people tell me it's necessary. The food is free. The wine is free. Nothing is free in this life. There's always a catch, always a price to pay.

"Anyway, it seems you enjoy this part of the job very much indeed, if not too much. But you have to understand, dear boy, that having fun and going to parties is not the job of a reporter. Not really.

"Your job is to get stories and tell stories, stories people want to read. Your job is to give people news they can use, information they can make sense of, and facts that make a difference. See what I'm saying?"

She was speaking so softly and kindly to me, like a grandmother with a good heart who doesn't want to upset her grandchildren by telling them they have misbehaved and disappointed her. I felt a lump forming in my throat. The kindness in her voice was touching.

"We can't have you merely playing at being a reporter. We need you to be a reporter, to do the real job of a reporter. We need you to get on with it, to just do the work."

She put her hand on mine and looked steadily into my eyes. A picture of my drunken departure from the victuallers' party popped into my mind. I saw myself staggering home in Rory's arms. I saw myself laughing and joking at the major's party.

There had been a lot more receptions since then, mostly ones Rory dragged me along to, not that I had ever resisted.

"So what are we going to do about it?" Miss Marlowe asked tenderly.

"I'm so sorry. I'll do better. I promise. I'll work harder. I'll change. I know I can change. I really love this job. I don't want to lose it."

"I know you don't want to lose it. We don't want you to go," said Miss Marlowe. "We like you. You are part of our team. We don't want you to go. But you must see how it looks to us - and by us, I mean how it looks to Ron and Harold, because they are the ones who came to me to share their concerns.

"All I want is for you to do your job, to the best of your ability, rather than gallivanting around, just playing at doing the job."

I couldn't speak. I was choked. Worse, I could feel tears forming in my eyes. I felt ashamed. I thought I had let Miss Marlowe down after all she had done for me.

She could see the serious look on my face. She could see how pale and distressed I was. I thought I was about to be sacked. I could see myself packing up my desk and walking out the front door with a cardboard box with nothing in it but a teacup.

"Okay, let's leave it there for today," Miss Marlowe said, pushing a handkerchief back into her pocket and taking another sip of water.

"You go and think about what we've talked about. I'll talk to Ron. I'll tell him we've spoken. He'll keep an eye on you. But please, remember what I said because we don't want to be forced to let you go. Go and make a fresh start, change your ways, and start taking the job more seriously."

As I left the room, I looked back. Miss Marlowe had her back to me, her head barely visible above the back of the armchair. The light from the fire flickered around her. I quietly closed the door behind me.

Ron looked up when I returned. I could tell he knew what had just happened. He nodded knowingly but said nothing.

In the following weeks, I did change. I worked harder. I stopped going with Rory to receptions I was not invited to. I concentrated on finding stories, worked longer hours writing stories, and cranked out more stories.

I invested more time in interviews. I added more information to stories, more detail, more quotes, and more background. I work weekends, covering events that were not on the diary.

Ron liked my new enthusiasm and even sent me a nice note saying how pleased he was with my progress and new work ethic.

I never knew if Miss Marlowe knew any of this. I don't know if she ever heard that I was trying harder, working more diligently, taking the job more seriously. I never got to find out.

One morning, I arrived at the office to find an ambulance outside. Mrs Partridge and Brenda were huddled together in the office doorway as they watched the ambulance drivers carrying a stretcher.

"Miss Marlowe?" I asked.

"Dead,' said Mrs Partridge.

Brenda began to weep. Mrs Partridge gave her a handkerchief. Mr Watson came out of the office and put his arm around Mrs Partridge.

"They found her in bed," he said. "She must have called the ambulance. Probably the last thing she did. The fire was still going. She was holding that damn book, you know, What it's Like to Die."

Mrs. Partridge pulled another handkerchief from her pocket and dabbed her eyes. The doctor came and wrote on the death notice: Natural causes.

Miss Marlowe was 82.

* * *

One of Ron's first acts as editor of The Messenger was to hire two new reporters, Jennifer Manners and Rodney Savage, both born and raised in Chesterton and graduates of the town's illustrious grammar school.

Ron moved into Dan's old spot, Jennifer took over Matthew's desk, and Rodney settled into Ron's old workspace. I insisted on staying where I was at my little dressing table desk. I had grown very fond of the cut-glass drawer handles, and I liked being close to Ron.

Jennifer was the daughter of the director of a local amateur dramatic society and had appeared in many of the group's productions. She was already well-known around town and was immediately assigned to cover the local theatre scene.

Rodney was an avid rugby player and talented cartoonist, the son of the art teacher at a secondary modern school. Ron thought Rodney would boost the paper's sports coverage and also contribute some of his cartoons to the paper.

Regardless of their education and accomplishments, Jennifer and Rod were still given the status of trainee reporters. This was great news for me as I was immediately set free from the tedious duties of fetching coke for the stove, taking parcels to the bus, and pinning photographs in the window.

Hallelujah.

* * *

CHAPTER THIRTY-TWO
GOLDEN

Fred Lester died fighting for the Derbyshire Fusiliers in France in the First World War. His body was never found. His name was inscribed on the cenotaph in the market square.

I knew all this because Fred told me himself when I went to interview him and his wife, Katie, about their golden wedding anniversary.

"They looked for me for months. They assumed I was dead," said Fred. "But I wasn't. I was in a camp for prisoners of war."

It was a chilly Tuesday morning in March that I sat with the Lesters in the snug living room of their Kirk Hallam home to talk about their 50 years of married life together.

I wanted to know all about the good times, the bad times, the ups, the downs, the happiest times, the sad days, the successes and disappointments. I asked them to tell me everything. They did, and I wrote it all down.

Stories about golden wedding anniversaries were popular with Messenger readers. We cover them as diligently as we cover council meetings and court cases.

Whenever someone came into the office to place a golden wedding notice, Brenda immediately handed the information to me, and I called the couple to arrange an interview and photograph. Golden wedding couples never refused.

"Get as much detail as you can," Ron told me as I headed off to see the Lesters. "We want to know where they met, how they felt at the time, where they married, how many kids they have, how many grandkids they have, we need to know all of it. And don't forget to ask them the most important question."

"The most important question?" I said.

"Yes," said Ron. "The most important question: How the hell did you manage to stay together for 50 years? We all really want to know the answer to that one."

My interview with the Fred and Katie Lester started, as I was to discover all interviews with golden-wedding couples would, with a warm and gushy welcome followed by an enthusiastic invitation to sit in the "best room", the tidiest room in the house, reserved and only used for special occasions.

Nothing was out of place in this room. Every item was perfectly placed, every surface immaculately dusted, every ornament polished to perfection. There was no clutter. Everything was spic and span, every item in its proper place, and the room always had a lingering odour of disinfectant and mothballs.

As I settled into an easy chair close to the fire, Katie carried in a tray of tea and biscuits. It had all been carefully thought out, and the tray was carried with pride and confidence and placed in plain view on a small table directly in front of us.

Milk was expertly poured into each cup. No questions were asked. It was assumed everyone took milk in their tea. Biscuits were offered on a plate. I took one, Fred took two. dipping one in his tea and placing the other on the rim of his saucer for later. Katie frowned at what she considered his bad manners but said nothing.

This was the typical and always pleasant start to any interview with a golden-wedding couple. Once the little ritual was completed, we could begin chatting about their life together over the last half century.

With the Lesters, Fred immediately told the story about his name being on the cenotaph. He laughed and repeated parts of the story, like him being in the prisoner of war camp more than once, just to make sure I had written it down. It was a story he loved and had obviously told often over the last 50 years.

"I worked at Cossall pit for years," said Fred. "Then, I worked as a bus driver. In 1939, I quit the buses and me and Katie opened a radio and electrical repair shop."

"It was never very good. We never made any money," said Katie. "We couldn't get parts. And people didn't want to pay. They thought our prices were too high."

Fred took up the conversation. They shared the storytelling like they would share a sandwich in a cafe.

"After a couple of years, we shut shop and opened a cafe instead," said Fred.

"That was too much work," said Katie. "We were putting in 18 hours a day and ending up with nothing for it."

"We had two little kids at that time," said Fred.

"It was a lot of work. We took the kids with us into the shop every day. They grew up there. We never took time off."

They talked and I wrote down every word as fast as I could. Years later, I realised that I didn't need to write down every word, only key dates, names and places. Rory once told me, "I never take notes. Most of what people say is rubbish. I can remember the important bits." But I was a stickler for writing everything down. I filled page after page of notebooks. A lot of it was illegible.

The Lesters were the typical golden-wedding couple. They were kind and soft spoken and couldn't resist looking over my shoulder every now and then to see what I was writing.

Their life of 50 years together seemed to go by in a flash. No sooner had they told me about their wedding day than they were telling me about grandkids and retirement.

I wrote down all the highlights of their life. Struggles to pay bills. Holidays by the seaside. Job changes. The time they saw the Queen. The day their dog got run over and a neighbour bought them a new one. The coming of grandchildren.

When I put my pen down, I couldn't believe how many pages I had filled. How time had galloped by, I thought. The room told a more complicated story. There were old photographs in frames. An heirloom clock on the mantlepiece. Treasured ornaments and souvenirs in a cabinet.

I looked at Fred and Katie and thought how well they seemed to fit together like two halves of an apple or hands pressed together in prayer.

When Fred spoke, I could see how carefully Katie listened and smiled, and how he did the same when she said something. It was more than politeness. It was an expression of gladness, a pleasure at seeing someone you like being happy.

When Katie poured the tea, Fred moved the milk jug out of the way and held a saucer in readiness to receive the cup.

When they moved around the room, they were ever conscious of where the other one was and made space for them, anticipating their every move. It was kindness acted out in the most straight-forward and ordinary actions.

It was love, although I never used that word, but I was aware of a deep, calm, gentleness and humility. I was touched by Fred and Katie's quiet dignity and willingness to always be helpful.

At the end of golden-wedding interviews, I always felt as if I had been in the presence of something good and worthy, something noble, a quality of life deserving of my respect and admiration.

Their 50 years together made me believe in the durability of love as well as the goodness that makes life meaningful and less dreary, shallow and crass.

"Before I go, I have to ask you the most important question," I said.

"We'll do our best to answer," said Katie.

"What's the secret to a long and happy marriage?"

"All know is that I like being with Katie," said Fred.

"Yes, we do like to be together," said Katie.

"I would sooner have tea and biscuits in front of the fire with her than be wined and dined at Buckingham Palace," said Fred.

"That would never happen," laughed Katie.

"But it's true. I would rather be with you doing whatever it is we are doing than be in a fancy restaurant."

"I think that's it," said Katie. "You have to be prepared to share. You can't have it all your own way all the time."

"We agree more than we disagree," said Fred. "We have never really argued, we just get on with it, and it all seems to work out."

"Does Fred always remember your birthday? Does he bring you flowers on Valentine's Day?" I asked.

"He remembers my birthday, but I can't remember the last time he brought me flowers for Valentine's," said Katie.

"Maybe I should start doing that," said Fred, and they both laughed.

As I said goodbye to the Lesters, Frank Skinner, our part-time photographer, arrived to take pictures.

He was always a little discombobulated, always seemed to be searching his pockets for lost keys. He carried a lot of equipment. A camera bag, an extra camera around his neck, and a couple of notebooks.

Frank was big on using ladders. He liked shots taken up high, looking down on his subject. His first question to a golden wedding couple was always the same: "Do you have a ladder?"

All of his golden wedding photos were the same. The couple, standing arm in arm, looking upward, holding their wedding photo from 50 years ago. He liked the idea that readers could see how the couple looked then and how they look today.

Sadly, time had not always been kind to many couples. I was often shocked when they opened the front door, and they were toothless, hairless, deathly pale, hunched over and wrinkly.

I started to make a point of looking into couples' eyes to try to see them as young people. It worked more often than not, and I could get a glimpse of how they were when they were young.

My golden-wedding stories always generated a positive response. I usually received a card or letter of appreciation. I propped the cards up on my desk and left them there for a week or two before tossing them into the waste basket.

* * *

CHAPTER THIRTY-THREE
UNFORGIVEN

Forgiveness is a very good thing for those who can do it. For those who can't, it can be a serious test of faith.

On the council housing estate in Kirk Hallam, kids were sword-fighting with bones they found on a wasteground.

They didn't know they were bones. Least of all, they had no idea they were playing with human bones, part of what was once a human skeleton.

Kids will be kids and do what kids do. These kids were out of school, wandering free as savages, picking over whatever they found on the wasteland.

When they came upon the long, hard, bony, stick-like things, they thought it would be fun to play at being pirates. They ended up duelling with human leg bones, using them as swords to fence with one another.

A young mother came to find what her son was doing and immediately recognised the bones as human.

"Put those down. And get away from there," she shouted at the kids and was promptly ignored. The kids carried on with their gruesome swordplay.

The mom grabbed her son by the hand and dragged him away. The other kids laughed and jeered and carried on playing.

The mother phoned the police. She also phoned us at the newspaper. I took the call. She bent my ear about how the town should be more careful about what it dumps and where it dumps it. She raged about how the kids had no idea what they were doing or what they were playing with. She said she was appalled that human remains could be discarded in such a disgraceful and insensitive way.

"There ought to be a law," she shouted down the phone.

"I think there is a law," I told her.

I wrote down her name and address and drove to the council house estate to see for myself what was going on. I didn't really believe everything she was saying. I imagined the kids had simply found a few tree branches that looked like bones.

At the wasteland, I found kids playing and I asked them about the bones. They took me to see where they were.

Our photographer, Frank Skinner, arrived with his giant bag of camera equipment and began taking photos of the kids as they used bones as swords.

One boy showed Frank how he had found a skull and arranged some bones around it to make a skull-and-crossbones.

"It's good, isn't it, Mister?' said the boy. "Just like a Jolly Roger."

It was a grisly sight. The kids were laughing, but we weren't. Police arrived and took charge, ordering the kids home and confiscating and bagging the bones, and telling me and Frank to clear off.

The young mom who phoned me came up and started berating me as if it were all my fault. The kids with big, goofy smiles, uncombed hair and dirt on their faces stood listening to what she was saying.

"The council thinks it can get away with anything," said the mom. "They just don't care. It would be different if this were some posh part of town," she said.

At the town hall, the clerk at the counter didn't believe what I was telling her.

"Are you serious? You're kidding, right?" she laughed.

"No, I'm not joking. This is serious. I've been out to Kirk Hallam and seen it for myself," I said. "All I want to know is the council responsible for dumping the bones there?"

The clerk could see I was serious. She flew into a panic and dashed away to the town clerk's office. Seconds later, she reappeared, accompanied by the town clerk who asked me for the exact location of the wasteground and a detailed account of what I'd seen.

He phoned the borough surveyor, who then called a contractor. It was confirmed that the bones must have come from St. John's churchyard, which was being renovated due to poor drainage.

"Workers have been excavating along the wall beside the church," said the town clerk. "They're putting in new pipes. It appears they dumped the soil they removed on the wasteground."

"I suspect the contractor was just trying to save money," said the town clerk. "He doubted he knew what was in the soil. I guess people had been buried there for centuries."

The man who operated the excavator told me he didn't see any bones in the soil when he loaded it onto the dump truck.

The dump truck driver told me he didn't see any bones when he dumped the soil at the waste ground.

"So no one's to blame," I said. The contractor shrugged. "Well, the bones came from somewhere."

The council confirmed that indeed the bones were from the graves next to the church. To me, this was all sensational stuff. I was excited that I had an exclusive, a great story that would make a gripping read.

My editor, Ron, agreed. He liked the story too, and he told me to do what he always told me to do: "Make sure you get as much detail as possible."

My next job was to talk to the Rev. Alan Roger, vicar of St. John's. I'd spoken to the police. I'd spoken to the town clerk. I'd interviewed the contractor, the excavator operator, the dump truck driver, the young mother and, of course, the kids.

Now it seemed perfectly reasonable that I needed to talk to the person in charge of the site where the bones came from: the vicar of St.John's Church.

I thought the Rev. Rogers would be pleased to see me, glad to hear what I had to tell him, and happy that I was alerting him to the problem. I was wrong. He was very unhappy. In fact, he was furious. When he saw me coming, he flew into a rage.

"How could you! How dare you!" he yelled at me as I walked up to the vicarage and gave him the news face to face.

"You've done a terrible thing! Do you realise what damage you've done!" he shouted, his face turning redder and spit spraying from his mouth.

I was shocked and taken aback by the force of his attack.

"I was just doing my job," I blurted. "I was following up on what a young mother told me. I'm just reporting the facts. I'm just saying what happened, what I saw with my own eyes."

The Rev. Rogers would not be placated. He was mad as hell, and he continued to rant and rage about the indecency of what I had done.

"This is a disgrace! You can't run a story about this!" he insisted. "You realise how many people you will be hurting? I intend to call your editor. I'll get you sacked for this."

I realised I needed to calm down and just get the answers to my questions. I asked him if he had been monitoring the renovation project. I wondered if he knew there were graves where the contractors had been digging.

He shook his head in anger and disgust. His nostrils flared, his cheeks puffed out, and his white hair was flying as if it were being blown by the wind. He waved his hands around manically, jabbed a finger at me, and kept saying over and over again what a terrible thing I was doing and how I had broken his trust.

"We are finished," he yelled. "I never wanted to lay eyes on you again."

At this point, I was upset myself. I was not used to being in such a nasty, aggressive confrontation. I backed away and stood frozen as I listened to the vicar rant. I could think of nothing to say in response.

There was only one voice being heard, and no space existed in the conversation for the voice of reason. I looked at the ground. I looked at the sky. I looked around to see if anyone was listening. I looked back at the Rev. Rogers, who was now insisting on an apology, demanding a promise that I would not write anything, and he reiterated his threat to call my editor and get me sacked.

I turned to leave. There was nothing more to say or do. As I began to walk back away, Rogers grabbed my arm and spun me around.

"I will never forgive you, never!" he said. "This is a despicable thing you're doing. No, I will never forgive you!"

For a moment, we both stood in silence. I looked at the wild-eyed vicar, seeing his angry face, red lips and wild, tousled hair. I couldn't believe what I was hearing, how he was behaving. Did he expect me to say I was sorry and to ask him to forgive me?

As a boy, I had sung in a church choir. I had listened to sermons. I knew nothing about church rules or laws, but I was pretty sure that forgiveness was a big deal.

"Can you say that?" I asked Rogers. "Can you say I won't forgive you? Isn't that against the rules?"

"Don't tell me about rules. You're breaking all the rules. I mean what I say. I won't forgive you. I'll never forgive you."

It didn't know my Bible, but I knew the story of the man who asked for his debt to be forgiven and then refused to forgive the debt of someone who owed him much less. As I looked at Rogers, I knew I was not looking into the face of love and compassion.

Back at the office, Ron had already had a similar conversation with Rogers on the phone.

Ron had promised him that the paper would be as sensitive as possible, but we needed to tell the story because it was something that should never have happened in the first place.

"I told him something must be done to prevent such a thing from happening again. When I asked him if he knew there were graves there, he slammed the phone down on me."

Ron instructed me to write the story, making sure to quote Rogers extensively as well as the town clerk, the borough survey, the contractor, the young mother, and the kids. I did exactly as I was told.

We ran the story. It got a big response from readers who mainly blamed the contractors and the town council for their negligence and incompetence.

The Rev. Rogers never spoke to me again. When he saw me in the town, he crossed the street. When he saw me at a meeting, he avoided eye contact. I felt unforgiven for years, but I never thought I had done anything wrong.

* * *

CHAPTER THIRTY-FOUR
ALLBRIGHT

Once a week, I was sent to write what Ron called a "puff piece" or a "people story." It was a feature rather than a hard-news story about some quirky aspect of life in the community.

It could be a 600-word piece on a group of ladies who get together every month to play Bridge. I would ask them about the art of bidding and winning tricks. Writing puff pieces was always educational. I learned something new, and it made a pleasant change of pace from covering council meetings and magistrates' court.

At his home in Vicarage Lane, Cotmanhay, the Rev. Dale Allbright, rector of Christ Church, was busy in the kitchen, preparing to siphon rosehip wine from one large demijohn into another. I had been dispatched to chat with the friendly vicar about his love of winemaking.

Set back from the street and hidden by maple trees and shrubs, the vicarage was hidden by a jungle of foliage.

The ramshackled Victorian house had large, bulging bay windows and a rustic wooden porch with a moss-covered roof.

A wave of wisteria swept over the brick facade. The vine's woody stems, held firmly in place by hooks, had been trained to climb up and over the bay windows, giving the house a slightly comical appearance, as if it had bushy eyebrows.

My route to the front door was through a squeaky iron gate, along a narrow path between overgrown hydrangeas and rhododendrons, under an arbour smothered by roses, and up to the cottage-style porch.

At the front door, I could hear music playing. A fan of Schubert, the Rev. Allbright was listening to the Trout Quintet as he fought to untangle a plastic hose for syphoning wine.

I stood and listened to the music for a few moments before ringing the doorbell. I heard footsteps, then the door opened, and I was greeted by a beautiful Japanese woman who knew who I was and why I was there.

"Hello, I'm Junko, you must be Steven from the Messenger," she said, smiled, bowed quickly, and waved me to come inside.

She invited me to leave my shoes by the front door and pick a pair of slippers from a pile in a wicker basket. This was all new and interesting to me. I had never been asked to remove my shoes before.

Junko said nothing but indicated that I should follow her down the corridor to the kitchen, where we found the Rev. Allbright still struggling with the thin plastic tubing.

"Ah, good," he said, brightly, "You're just in time to give me a hand with this darn thing. It is always getting tangled."

He handed me one end and told me to walk backwards until the tubing was stretched out and untangled.

"I see you've met Junko," he said.

"Is she your housekeeper?" I asked.

"Housekeeper! Oh no, she's my wife," said Allbright, and he laughed. Junko laughed, too. I could feel my face turning red.

"That's okay," said Junko, speaking perfect English. "You're not the first to assume I'm the hired help."

"I'm so sorry," I squirmed. "That's not the first time I've put my foot in it. My editor says I should never assume because . . . "

"Because it makes an ass of you and me," said Junko,

completing my thought. "Yes, it's true, but not to worry, we all do it."

She laughed again, and I was struck by how pretty and affirming the sound of her laughter was and how quick she had been to see the funny side of my asinine assumption.

"Junko and I met two years ago in Kyoto," said Allbright. "I was there on sabbatical, studying Buddhism and Shinto from an ecumenical perspective. Junko was one of our guides."

He fed the siphon tube into the glass jug of rosehip wine.

"It was love at first sight. Just like the Beatles say in their song, 'Would you believe in a love at first sight? Yes, I'm certain that it happens all the time.' We spent a week going around Kyoto together, visiting temples and gardens and talking about love and life. I proposed the same week."

Junko put her hand on Allbright's shoulder as a gentle way of letting him know she was going to interrupt him.

"I didn't say yes right away," she said. "I needed to talk to my parents first. They live in Hiroshima. I went there to see them and explain what happened. They didn't know what to think."

Allbright jumped back into the conversation.

"Ah, but once we met and they could see how much I loved their daughter, how much in love we both were, well, they gave us their blessing.

"We were married the next week on Miyajima by a priest on the course with me. And that's the short version of our story. My Japanese isn't good, but Junko's English is excellent. Thank God for that."

Junko kissed Allbright gently on the cheek and smiled at me before leaving the room, all the time insisting that I should come back to visit them in the summer for tea in the garden.

Allbright came back to the job at hand: the racking of the rosehip wine, separating it from the thick layer of sediment in the demijohn.

"Okay, I think we're ready to start racking," said Allbright, flashing me a toothy grin.

"Racking?"

"Just another way of saying siphoning. We're going to use gravity to push the wine from this jar into the smaller jar down here on the floor. It'll only take a minute or two.

"The Romans used gravity to get water to fill their aqueducts from the mountains. It's a simple principle. I'm also using air pressure to push the wine into the tube and down into this jar. Marvellous, isn't it? No machines, no pumps, no mechanisms, just natural science. I love it."

When Allbright spoke, there was a warmth and cheerfulness in his voice. His eyes sparkled with such enthusiasm and he never stopped smiling. I could see he had a gift for communicating. He never came across as arrogant or condescending.

As the last drop of wine dribbled into the jar, Allbright lifted the hose, shook it and dumped it in the sink.

"Okay, let's take this wine to the basement. It's nice and cool there," he said. I followed him down creaky stairs into a cellar where there were rows of demijohns full of different coloured wines and shelves stacked with wine bottles.

"See this machine? It's for corking," he said excitedly. "You place the bottle here, pull this lever, and Bob's your uncle, the cork gets pushed into the bottle. I think it is fantastic. So simple."

I pointed at other interesting items on the shelves.

"Those are plastic caps. You slip them over the top of bottles. They shrink and make the bottle look very professional.

"I have fancy labels, too. I like my bottles to look like they're from a French chateau. It's just a bit of fun. I'm not really trying to fool anyone. It's just a way to make the finished bottle look more attractive."

He pointed to other pieces of equipment: a hydrometer, funnels, and fermentation airlocks. The words were all new to me. Now, he was speaking very quickly, and I struggled to keep up as I jotted down notes. I kept telling him to slow down and hold on a minute.

"What do you do with all this wine?" I asked.

"Drink it!" he laughed. "No, that's not true. We drink some of it. With friends mostly. I give a lot away, as gifts, when we go to a party or to a parishioner's home for dinner."

He thought for a second about what he'd just said and laughed.

"Well, let's say I give my wine away. It doesn't mean the people I give it to want it." And he laughed. "They never say no, and I've never had any complaints, so it can't be that bad.

"It's all magical, I reckon. A kind of alchemy. I mean, this is all about turning water into wine, if you'll pardon the reference. You take a simple ingredient, like rosehips, pears or rhubarb, add water, pop in a little yeast, and Bob's your uncle, the next thing you know, whoosh, you've got a lovely wine to drink. Magic!"

Back in the kitchen, Allbright looked at his watch and checked its accuracy against the clock on the wall.

"Ah, good, it's noon. Let's have a taste, shall we? Now, let's see, you should try some of my best rosehip. I think it's delicious."

He pulled the cork from the bottle. It made a loud pop. He smiled, happy that the cork came away in one piece, and then he poured the light rose-coloured liquid into two plain wine glasses.

Before tasting, he lifted his glass and held it in the shafts of warm light streaming in through the window.

"I love the colour of this wine. It's such a warm, soft pink, and the bouquet is delightful. It's a very earthy wine. It has the smell of a garden. Well, it would, wouldn't it, after all, it came from the roses in my garden."

I took a sip. I didn't like the taste. It was too dry and bitter for me, but I gave two thumbs up. I didn't consider this to be lying. I was simply being encouraging and supportive. What did I know about wine anyway, I thought.

For a moment, neither of us said anything. We just stood in

the kitchen, sipping the wine, listening to the ticking of the clock on the wall, and admiring the bright shafts of sunshine streaming through the window.

"Come on," said Allbright. "It's too nice to be stuck in here. Let's take our glasses into the garden. The sun's out and it looks glorious."

He pushed open French doors and stepped into the garden, which I now realised was much bigger than I had first imagined.

Allbright took a deep breath and exhaled, lifted his head, closed his eyes and let the sunshine brighten his face.

"Ever heard of the Rev. Eli Jenkins from Under Milk Wood?" he asked. I shook my head.

"Well, he's a vicar who comes out of his house every morning and says a prayer to the town. It's hilarious and beautiful. He says: 'We are not wholly bad or good/ Who live our lives under Milk Wood/ And Thou, I know, wilt be the first,'To see our best side, not our worst.' Isn't that lovely? 'To see our best side, not our worst.' I love it.'

We walked to a small table and two chairs in a grove of apple trees.

"All my rosehips come from here. I collect them from the end of August to November," said Allbright.

"I get a few from the neighbours, but I prefer to use my own because they come from old rose varieties. I think they have more flavour."

He talked about his winemaking tools. He talked about the art of washing rosehips. He went on about pectic enzymes. I was overwhelmed. He spotted the fatigue on my face and stopped.

"Oh dear, I'm sorry. I got carried away. I'm talking too much. Mea culpa. Forgive me. Anyway, you get the idea. I think you've got enough to be going on with.

"Just remember, you can make wine from pretty much anything: dandelions, rhubarb, parsnips, beets, celery, plums, elderberry."

We emptied our glasses and got up to stroll some more.

"This garden was started by the rector before me. He loved roses and planted all old garden varieties like Madame Alfred Carriere, William Lobb, Fantin Latour, Charles de Mills and Souvenir de la Malmaison. I've added a few more."

These were all unfamiliar names to my ear. They sounded beautiful, foreign and exotic.

It was early spring. The roses were not yet in bloom, but Allbright knew all the plants even without seeing flowers. The ground was carpeted by blue bells, and we had to step carefully to avoid crushing them.

"These are English bluebells," said Allbright. "Spanish ones are more common, but they're upright, more erect, more stately. English ones are shy. They droop their heads to one side. I like both kinds, but the English ones are my favourite. They make me think of Junko. She's a little shy, you know."

Birds were skipping through the trees. A robin. A blackbird. Some starlings. Lots of sparrows. A few finches. Sunlight pushed through the canopy of the trees and created shadowy patterns and shapes on the grass. Allbright was still talking about roses.

"The only downside to these particular roses is that they bloom only once," he explained. "They give you everything they have, and when they're finished, they stop. That's it, they're done.

"Old garden roses will knock your socks off with their fragrance. They're so scented, it can be intoxicating just being close to them.

"You should come back in June and see what I mean. The garden is spectacular then. The air is so sweet. It's literally saturated with scent. You can smell the roses before you even get through the front gate."

"Do you have a favourite?" I asked. "One you simply could not live without?"

"An impossible question. They're all gems. 'Complicata', a Gallica rose, is special. It has a simplicity, an uncomplicated, open-faced honesty, an elegant beauty like no other. I like it a lot.

It's also a beautiful pink. Junko loves Complicata, too. I guess it's our special rose."

I said I should be writing about his garden and love of roses instead of wine-making.

"Why not do both. Come back and I'll show you the garden at its peak when all the roses are in full bloom. You could write about the roses.

"I always tell people if I were to die here in this garden in the middle of summer, I wouldn't even know I was dead."

He looked sideways at me to see if I had a clue what he was talking about. I did not.

"You see, I wouldn't know I was dead because the transition from here to heaven would be imperceptible. In this rose garden, I'm already in paradise."

As we returned to the house, I said I'd like to ask him a question about forgiveness.

"Forgiveness? My, that's a big topic. Where did that come from?" he said.

I told him about my encounter with the Rev. Rogers and how he had said he would never forgive me.

"Yes, I heard about your story. Too bad more care wasn't taken. But, hey, no use crying over spilt milk.

"There is always forgiveness. We all deserve a second chance. What do I tell people here week after week: Forgive us our trespasses as we forgive those who trespass against us.

"Don't worry, there's always forgiveness. But it sounds to me like you may need to forgive poor Alan. I mean, it works both ways, you know, this forgiveness business. We have to do it if we want others to forgive us."

On my way to the front door, I noticed a basket filled with tiny paper birds.

"They're origami cranes. Junko folds them," said Allbright. "She's folded hundreds of them. She teaches origami at the church and hands out these paper birds at services. Kids like to take them home."

Junko appeared from a back room. She bowed again and said goodbye, and as she did, she reached into the basket of paper cranes, picked out a beautiful blue one and handed it to me.

"Peace to you," she said. 'Put it on your desk at the office. It'll be a nice reminder of your visit."

"If you fold a thousand of these birds, you get to make a wish," said Allbright. "I think Junko has folded enough for several wishes."

We shook hands, and I left feeling very positive. As I went, Allbright recited another few lines of poetry.

"And not by eastern windows only

When daylight comes, comes in the light,

In front, the sun climbs slow, how slowly,

But westward, look, the land is bright."

The Rev. Allbright and Junko became my friends. I visited them many times, often with friends.

The Allbrights always gave us wine, and honey on bread, and Junko never let us leave without giving everyone a paper crane.

I forgave the Rev. Rogers. I hope he was able to forgive me.

* * *

CHAPTER THIRTY-FIVE
MO

It was while I was working in Chesterton that I bought my first car, a green 1958 Morris Minor 1000. I paid 80 pounds for it. It had four doors, still ran perfectly despite its age, and didn't have a scratch or a dent on it, having been owned by an elderly lady who bought it brand new and rarely used it.

I knew nothing about cars or the significance of low mileage. All I knew was that Mo, as I called the car, started straight away, sounded fantastic and purred along as if it loved being out on the road going places.

I loved everything about Mo. The colour. The shape. The smell of the worn leather seats. The tiny boot. The pop-up hood. The wind-down windows. The hilarious trafficators, little turn semaphore signals, that popped out from the sides.

For me, Mo meant freedom from having to wait for buses, an end to the frustration of it taking hours to get places, and a satisfying release from the awkward and uncomfortable business of having to rely on others to take me where I need to go.

The moment I got Mo, I started to travel. I motored into the countryside. I drove to the Peak District and walked the hills. I went to Matlock and Chatsworth. I travelled to Glossop,

Bakewell and Chapel-en-la-Frith. I visited Ripley, Belper and Heanor for the first time.

I was amazed at how much I could do and see on a simple day trip. I especially enjoyed stopping in a village, parking Mo, and walking to a pub for lunch or into a shop to buy an ice cream. It was all new and exciting to me.

Soon after I got Mo, Ron thought it would be good if I studied typing and shorthand, and he enrolled me in a secretarial course at the local college.

It was a one-day-a-week session in a class of about 30 young women, all of whom were desperate to become secretaries and personal assistants and needed excellent typing skills as well as fast Pitman shorthand.

I was the only male in the classroom. I was not embarrassed. Quite the reverse. The female teacher introduced me as the star reporter with the local newspaper, and this went down very well with my fellow classmates.

I didn't learn Pitman's shorthand. It was just too difficult. I can't say I tried very hard. I was more interested in getting to know my new study companions and impressing them with my vast experiences as a reporter.

My typing skills didn't improve much either. I started well, using all my fingers to do the recommended exercise, banging out a-s-d-f-g and h-j-k-l over and over again, but it was not my idea of fun.

My Mondays were mainly spent flirting. It didn't take long before I managed to persuade some of the girls to take the day off and come joyriding with me into the Derbyshire hills.

Three girls were especially keen. They never stopped giggling and talking as we tootled along in my little car into the lush green Derbyshire countryside.

Sometimes, we did what I loved doing, stopping in a pretty village and finding a beautiful spot by a stream or a picturesque view for lunch. We had a wonderful time. I enjoyed being the driver, and the girls loved skipping out of class.

This happy period didn't last long. The teacher soon noticed her missing students. Harsh words were spoken. The girls changed their ways and became conscientious again, and began to give me the cold shoulder.

I felt I needed to make them a better offer. I suggested we take a trip to the seaside. To Skegness, Mablethorpe or Ingoldmells. I made it sound fabulous. A day by the sea, fun riding donkeys, playing in the penny arcade, and buying Kiss Me Quick hats. Sadly, they would have none of it

Mondays in the classroom became very tedious. The girls had been read the riot act, and they were determined to stick to their guns and resist any distractions from me.

I tried one last change of tactics. It was a big move. I decided to change my name. I told the girls I had decided to change my name to Hayden Royale and pursue a career as a poet.

I had been introduced to the poetry of John Clare and William Wordsworth and was in love with the sound of nature poems.

At tea breaks, I would regale them with poems I'd quickly dashed off about the beauty of the countryside.

"Tired of the race, he, the country to embrace, travelled with speed with ease of mind into a field of a common kind, there to commune with the trees and the sky."

It was rubbish and it didn't impress. I switched my style and started cranking out what I called pop poetry. I invented a lonely, sad character called P. Duckheart who could never keep a girlfriend. I thought love and loneliness would do the trick.

The Love Song of P. Duckheart
Yester one way, some say, sun gay, Tuesday aftergloom
P. Duckheart Beatled his weary way,
across a dreary tone-deaf day
to meet glamour glitter, babysitter
Poly Propolene.
Whist lingering, loose-change tickling
jingling. tic tac toe,

> Duckheart criss-crossed Market Square
> counting pigeons in the air,
> until he spotted glamour-glitter, babysitter
> Poly Pro-pop-scene
> But love is quick and love is clean
> and love is often in-between
> for racing car-like, shooting star-like,
> cut-glass sparkle, cocktail-bar-like
> Pretty Poly, disco dolly, turned at LP speed
> and moving like a champagne cork,
> glamour-flittered down Exchange Walk
> Yester one-way, some say sun-gay
> Tuesday after-gloom, broken
> Duckheartless sat silent
> and breathless, and
> cried himself
> sense,
> less anyone should stop
> and ask him his name.
> Anyone.

None of this worked. The girls laughed. I cried. No, not really. But I soon realised they were not laughing with me. I guess I was more like Duckheart than I had realised.

* * *

CHAPTER THIRTY-SIX
ANNIE

Just when I thought my fun-Monday days were all done and dusted and I would never meet a girl who would find me the slightest bit interesting, Annie McLeod came into my life.

She was studying art history and learning to paint with watercolours and oils, and I first spotted her holding court with her art-loving buddies in the college refectory.

"Point to anyone in the room and I will tell you their star sign and all about their life," she told her pals. They pointed to me as I sat alone at the other end of the room, huddled over a hot bowl of tomato soup.

"Hmm, let me see," she said, studying me from a distance. "Sad, lonely, shy, but complicated. A little unsociable, a little mysterious, a person who spends a lot of time on his own. A Scorpio for sure. Yes, most definitely, Scorpio."

Annie's friends laughed.

"Possibly a sex maniac," she added. Her friends laughed some more.

"Go on, ask him," one of them told her.

"Okay, I will."

She walked up to my table bold as brass, sat down with one foot up on the chair next to her, said nothing, and watched me spooning soup from my bowl.

"We're having a bet that I can guess your star sign," she said. "I said Scorpio. I'm right, yes?"

"Wrong," I said. "Taurus the bull."

"No, that can't be right. Stubborn. Conservative. Stick-in-the-mud. Bit of a temper. You don't look at all like a Taurus," said Annie.

"I have a thick neck," I said. "Don't all Tauruses have a bull's neck? My turn. Let me guess your sign. I'd say, Aries. Quick-to-judge. Brash. Headstrong. Creative. Unpredictable."

"Wrong," laughed Annie. "Cancer. Imaginative. Creative. Loyal. Ambitious. Yes, I can definitely be headstrong and unpredictable."

"Sounds perfect to me," I said. "Pleased to meet you."

Annie described herself as a "mature student", which meant she was over 20 and attending the art classes of her own volition, not because she was being paid by an employer or her parents were making her.

She took me to meet the other "mature students" in her group. In no time at all, we had all become friends. I started going to college every day just to see Annie.

We would sit in the refectory, drinking tea, and talking about art and poetry. We would tell stories about our lives, about people we knew, and I would talk about my job as a reporter, and she would tell me about her ambition to become a painter with a studio and shop. Sometimes, we would sit and talk for hours, all afternoon, until it was time for the refectory to close.

Annie loved the Impressionists. I had never heard of them before I met Annie. She seemed to know everything about them and the Impressionism movement.

She flipped open a book and pointed out page after page of glorious paintings by Monet, Renoir, Pissarro, Cassatt and Sisley. Annie loved them all, especially Monet.

It was a whole new world to me. I was seeing images for the first time that made me see everything in a whole new, exciting way. It was all wonderful. I was thrilled, and wondered I why this fantastic epiphany, this delightful awakening, had taken so long to happen.

The way I felt about seeing the paintings for the first time was the same way I felt about being with Annie. It felt like walking in the sunshine of a wheat field in summer after being locked away in the dark days of winter.

Annie brought her friends to my house on Market Street. We made tea and ate toast and honey, listened to music and opened more books on art.

We looked at paintings by Leonardo da Vinci, Brueghel, Caravaggio, Rembrandt, Vermeer and Picasso, but we always came back to the paintings we all love most, those of the French Impressionists.

I said I liked Van Gogh, Seurat, and Cezanne, far more than Degas, but Annie was quick to point out that they were all technically post-Impressionists, artists who came after Monet had invented Impressionism.

"Van Gogh and Cezanne and the others were inspired by the Impressionists, but they came later and were different," she said. I bowed to her superior knowledge, but I still loved paintings by Van Gogh more than those by Degas.

Annie wanted me to love Cezanne as much as she did.

"Look at the way Cezanne uses light and colour," she rhapsodised. "Look at his use of shapes and the simplicity of his subjects. I mean, apples on a table, how direct, how dramatic, how simple is that. Isn't it beautiful?"

And I look into her face, framed by her lovely cascading blonde hair, and found it impossible to disagree.

"Beautiful," I said. "Full of light and life."

"Anyway, why do you like Van Gogh so much?" she asked.

"I don't like every painting. I like this one," I said, pointing at Wheatfield with Crows in her book.

"I like the way the path takes you deeper into the wheat while black crows are flying all around overhead. It's so intense. It makes me feel sad. To be alone in a field with crows flying over you."

"It would annoy me. I hate crows," said Annie.

I could see she liked what I had to say, and she turned the page and showed me more Van Gogh paintings, including Starry Night, Sunflowers, and Cafe Terrace at Night.

One image jumped out at me and stayed in my mind. It was The Sower, a picture of a man sowing seeds in a field just as the sun comes up.

"He's all alone, but he doesn't care because he's doing something wonderful. Putting seeds into the ground. I love that," I said. Annie was amused and a little impressed that I liked it so much.

"You know it's a copy?" she said. "Millet did it first. And better in my opinion." She flipped deeper into her book and found a photo of The Sower by Jean-Francois Millet.

"See, it's a copy," she said, smiling.

"I don't care. It was probably what inspired Van Gogh to do his painting. I still like Vincent's Sower more."

Annie was touched by my defence. I noticed she looked even more beautiful with her face filled with light and her long blonde hair falling freely to her shoulders and touching her pretty, flowered blouse.

"You know Van Gogh was mad, totally bonkers?" she said.

"Mad about art? I can see that," I said. "What I see is passion and honesty, a love of things beautiful, a love for simple things just as they are."

Annie turned the pages back to a painting by Monet.

"These are good, too," I said, and she laughed.

"Well, how very nice of you to say," she mocked.

Annie stayed behind when everyone left my house. We opened a bottle of wine, put on music by Joni Mitchell and Don

McLean, and sat in front of the fire, looking at more art in her books.

I lit some candles and read Annie some of my daft poems, and laughed and said they were terrible, and why did I bother.

She told me about her paintings and showed me some photos that she had in her purse. They were all Cezanne-style landscapes with paint applied in patches and blotches and streaks and always with soft, muted colours.

I made her laugh again by saying her paintings were like Cezanne's and a bit like Monet's.

We spent a lot of time together in the weeks that followed, going here and there in my car, Mo. We were in love, but we never said so. We were boyfriend and girlfriend, but we never announced it.

We went to the Peak District for picnics. We visited the Allbrights and had tea with them in their garden, and walked around smelling the roses.

Allbright was right. The air was indeed saturated with their perfume in summer. We could smell the roses the moment we walked through the front gate.

Annie and I also visited Haddon Hall and Chatsworth House to see the gardens, the fountain, and the cascades, and we went to Newstead Abbey to see where Byron had lived, although we ended up liking the gardens most of all.

Annie lectured me all the way there and back about the Romantic poets and Byron in particular, and how he died fighting for the Greeks.

It all went in one ear and out the other, but Annie was passionate about it and kept on until I agreed that it was a noble thing for Byron to give up his life for others.

As a result of our visit to Newstead, Annie reluctantly agreed to come along to one of the poetry nights I organised once a month at the Dog and Duck Inn on Bath Street. Dylan Bishop and the others were always there.

Annie came, but she laughed too much. She laughed at the wrong times, and some of the poets took umbrage.

"You're banned," I told her.

"You can't ban me!" she protested. "Anyway, I never wanted to come in the first place."

"Well, you're still banned," I said.

She laughed.

Annie became a fixture at my house on Market Street. I gave her a key, and she was often there when I got home from work. Sometimes, she brought groceries and cooked a meal. Sometimes, she brought friends.

She always felt free to invite whomever she liked, and she stayed as long as she wanted. She never moved in, but she stayed over most nights.

Her actual home was with her parents in a big house in Kimberley, a town only a short way from Chesterton. She was an only child, and her parents were rich.

I was shocked when she eventually took me to her house, and I realised for the first time just how wealthy her parents were.

The house was a large, Tudor-style mansion with many rooms, including a study, library and conservatory with all sorts of hothouse plants. It also had a large garden with topiaries, manicured lawns, and classy boxwood parterres.

Annie showed me around and pointed to a barn at the back of the house, where there was a fenced paddock.

"This is where I keep my horse," she said.

"Your horse! You have a horse?" I gasped. "How come you never mentioned it?"

"It's not important," she said. "Who cares? My dad bought it for me years ago when I was a kid. I'm not into horses anymore. Art is what I love now. Art and handsome reporters."

She explained that the house had been in the family for years and sat on ten acres of land.

"My dad's an architect. He likes to have lots of space. He needs a lot of space. Just like me," she said.

Weeks passed. Annie and I saw less and less of one another as she became more involved with her art group at the college.

Her dad got her a shop, which she turned into a studio, and exhibited all her paintings, oils, and watercolours. They were good. I loved them, but could never afford to buy them.

I was still preoccupied with my job at the paper, my weekly routines, my assignments, attending magistrates' court, council meetings, cranking out football and wedding reports, and deciphering the pigeon news.

It had become my life. It was my routine, and it gave me stability and a feeling of worth as well as an income. I liked it.

People at the office had become my family. I still popped into Stan's for a fried egg sandwich, and he still curses at me every time.

Ron had become my friend as well as my editor. I often went to his house for lunch, and he had introduced me to his wife, Patricia.

I saw Rory all the time. We went to the pub together, he came to poetry nights, and I resumed going with him to promotions and events where they served free food and drinks.

All this routine was not easy for Annie to accept. She found it tedious, restricting, and boring. She was more interested in her artistic friends at the college.

Her family took her away for weeks at a time to Spain and France. We started to see each other less and less.

The last time we were together was on a day trip with her art class to London to visit the National Gallery.

I jumped at the chance to spend the day with Annie, looking at paintings by Monet and Van Gogh and visiting famous pubs like the Lamb and Flag. Sadly, that was not to be.

Annie had fallen in love with someone in her art class. On the day trip to the National, I spent most of my time only own, looking at Turner and Constable paintings.

Annie's tastes had changed, too. She was no longer into Impressionism. Now, she liked the Dutch masters.

She didn't laugh when I said Vermeer was all surface and no substance. But we both still shared a love of Monet and his water lilies.

Weeks later, I heard Annie had left the college and moved to Spain. I never saw her again.

CHAPTER THIRTY-SEVEN
SIDES

On the edge of town, old, neglected houses on Rupert Street that were showing their age with flaking stucco facades, sunken, collapsing roofs and broken, dirty windows.

Marilyn and Martin Shaw, a young married couple about to have their first child, were living in one of the houses. They called me out of desperation. "Come and see what we're having to put up with," said Marilyn. "You come and see the filth we're having to live with, the awful conditions we're expected to bring our a new baby into."

I drove to Rupert Street. The Shaws were living at No.6. I knocked on the door, and Marilyn answered and showed me into the living room, which was scruffy with its threadbare carpet and uneven, crumbling floors.

In the kitchen, water ran dark and dirty into the sink from a crooked and tarnished tap.

The upstairs toilet didn't flush properly and frequently overflowed. There was a disgusting, decaying smell in one of the bedrooms, as if a bird or rat had died under the floorboard or was trapped inside the walls.

"We have to keep going to the pub at the end of the street to use the toilet," said Marilyn. "Sometimes they tell us it's not convenient and tell us to use the one at the petrol station."

Marilyn was six months pregnant and already moving awkwardly as he moved gingerly from room to room.

In the master bedroom, there was a tatty mattress on the floor with a pillow propped up against the wall at one end. There was no mattress. No bed frame. Just the mattress on the floor.

"This is where we sleep. We can't afford anything better. We have no money," said Martin. "I lost my job at the factory months ago. Now we have to live on what I get every week from the dole."

Marilyn rolled her eyes. She had heard Martin's tale of woe many times by the look of it.

"How can we bring our baby into this slum?" she asked, her voice cracking with indignation.

"We contacted the council, but they refuse to help us. They wouldn't even talk to us. They won't lift a finger."

She started to cry. She was pale and looked unwell, and her ill-fitting floral dress made her look even sadder and more pathetic.

I sat and listened to their tale of frustration and rejection. I wrote down every word, noting every deficiency in the house - the cracked window frames, broken floorboards, holes in the roof, leaking taps, non-flushing toilet, and awful smell in the bedroom.

"When it rains, water comes in there and runs down the wall," said Martin. "I tried to fix it, but it didn't last. The rain still comes in."

I was appalled by everything I had seen and heard. I listened with as much compassion and sympathy as I could muster, and when I left, I promised that I would do everything in my power to help.

"You can trust me," I said. "I'm on your side. This is an

absolute disgrace. No one should have to live like this. It's inhumane. The council should be ashamed of itself."

In a dark and angry mood, I stomped back into the office. I yanked the cover from my typewriter, sat down, pushed copy paper into the roller, and began feverishly pounding on the keys.

Ron noticed my aggressive, agitated typing and asked me what I was working on. I told him the basic details.

A young married couple, soon to be parents, forced to live in poverty and squalor while the town council turns a deaf ear and does nothing. Taps spewing filthy water. Toilets won't flush. Roof leaking. Rats rotting in the walls. No coal for the fire. A mattress on the floor for a bed. I went on and on. Ron lifted his hand to stop me.

"Have you talked to the council?" he asked.

"No. But look at the conditions they're living in. It's not right. It's outrageous. It's diabolical."

"Yes, yes, but you need to hear the other side," said Ron.

"Other side? What other side? There's no other side. Marilyn is six months pregnant. Martin doesn't have a job. The house is an appalling slum. What other side could there be?"

"Call the town hall," said Ron. "See what they have to say. Then write your story. You always need to hear the other side. Okay?"

Albert Brown, in the housing department at the town hall, took my call and immediately knew the houses I was talking about when I mentioned Rupert Street.

"Yes, there are six houses there. All unoccupied, but one," Brown said. "We're well aware of the situation."

I launched into my tirade. How could the council be so uncaring? How could they treat people in such a disgraceful, heartless way? Was he aware that Marilyn Shaw was six months pregnant? Did he realise Martin Shaw was unemployed, having lost his job months ago?

"Wait, wait, wait," Brown cried down the phone. "Hold your horses. We are talking about No.6, correct?

"Yes, " I said impatiently. "No.6. The Shaws."

"Okay, well, we have approached them several times," said Brown. "We've had someone from the engineering department go, let me see, at least three times."

"What for?" I interjected. "To fix the toilets? To fix the roof. To remove the dead rats from the walls?" I said sarcastically.

"No, no. To inform them that the place is condemned and unfit for habitation, and they can't live there due to health and safety concerns. We have plans to demolish all the houses on that street at the end of the month."

"What about the Shaws? " I demanded. "What happens to them?"

"Well, they are technically squatters right now," said Brown. "They shouldn't be there. They know this. We have told them they are breaking the law. But they refuse to go.

"Go where?" I said.

"Go to the new council house we've offered them up the street. We told them they can move in whenever they're ready. It's a new house, never been occupied. It had all the modern fixtures. Bathroom. Kitchen. Stove. Everything is brand new."

I was silent.

"Are you still there?" Brown asked.

"Yes, I'm here. Why would they refuse to leave?" I asked.

"Mystery to me," said Brown. "They have a bee in their bonnet about us not caring and refusing to fix the house. I think Mrs Shaw wants to live close to her mother."

"Her mother?" I said. "They never said anything about that."

"No, they didn't tell us at first. But that's what the issue is, as we understand it. Mrs Shaw won't move out because she wants to stay close to her mother, who lives up the street."

I was silent again. The Shaws had mentioned none of this.

"Why don't they just go and live with her mother?" I said.

It was Mr. Brown's turn to be silent. I pressed the point again.

"I mean, it must be better than where they are living," I said.

"Can't they just move in with Marilyn's mother until the baby is born and they know what they want to do?"

"You should ask them. We can't figure it out either. We're as baffled as you are. We keep asking them to be reasonable, to take the new house, to move out. They just won't listen. We have served them with an eviction order. They ignore everything we say.

"If they don't move, we will be forced to move them out with the help of the police at the end of the month. That's when we'll demolish the houses. They're just not safe. They've been condemned for ages."

I tried to think of what else I could say.

"And you've offered them a new house?"

"Yes, a new council house in Gordon Street, just around the corner. They can move in anytime," Brown said. "They even get a free month's rent. It's part of the agreement when you move in. And the rent is very low. We've even offered to help find Mr Shaw a job. All he has to do is come to the Unemployment Office."

As I put down the phone, I turned to see that Ron had been listening behind me all the time. He said nothing. He just smiled weakly, knowing that he had been right all along that there was, indeed, another side to the story.

I grabbed my coat and told Ron I was off to see the Shaws to tell them what I had learned.

"Make it snappy," said Ron. "We've other work to do."

When I got to Rupert Street, the Shaws were climbing into a taxi with all their clothes stuffed into bundles of plastic bags.

I caught up with them just as they were closing the door of the taxi. Marilyn rolled the back window down to speak to me. Martin ignored me and looked out the other window.

"We're going to my mother's, up the street," she said. "We can't stand it here any longer."

I was silent.

"Thanks for your help. It was nice talking to you. I don't think we need the story now," she yelled as the taxi pulled away.

I watched as the taxi disappeared, leaving a trail of smoke. I turned to look at the house with its dirty windows and wonky roof and garbage strewn on the wasteland at the side.

A gang of boys started throwing stones to smash windows. The glass cracked and fell to the ground with a crash.

* * *

CHAPTER THIRTY-EIGHT
PRESTON

In September 1971, as part of my training, the Messenger sent me on a three-month journalism course to a college in Preston, Lancashire.

The idea was for me to improve my skills, learn a new, exciting and easier form of shorthand called T-line, and to engage with other reporters in lively discussions about how to write stories and tell the news.

In Preston, I met reporters from Liverpool and from other towns and suburbs around Merseyside, including Formby, Crosby, and Bootle.

Other reporters came from Manchester, Stockport, Burnley and Bury. I was forced to share rented digs with an angry Scotsman who wore too much Brut aftershave and made my life a living hell by jumping out of bed every morning and turning his radio to heavy metal rock music. I survived, but only just.

In Liverpool, I went with my new friends to the Philharmonic Hall to listen to Ted Hughes read his poems and afterwards to the Big House for umpteen pints of beer.

Liverpool was a frequent destination. I got to take the ferry across the Mersey, visited the Cavern Club, saw the Liver Building up close, and hung out in the Big House on Lime Street.

It was while I was at the college in Preston that I first heard the poetry of Liverpool poets Roger McGough and Adrian Henri.

I loved their poetry. Everything about it. The humour, directness, simplicity, earthiness, and the everyday, working-class images and language.

I marvelled at the creativity and inventiveness of these gifted, entertaining poets. McGough told the amusing but poignant story, such as the one about a priest in a fish and chip queue, wondering, as the vinegar runs through, how nice it would be to buy supper for two. Henri wrote fabulous love poems. "Love is walking holding paint-stained hands," he wrote. It was music to my ears. Where had these poets been all my life, I thought.

Preston was not far from Liverpool, so it was easy for me to contact the talented Mersey poets. I wanted to know them better.

I went to Liverpool to meet them, first Roger McGough, then Adrian Henri. Both were very friendly. They graciously welcomed me into their homes when I knocked at their front door. It was as easy as that.

I persuaded them to come to Preston to join a bunch of us at the college who were putting on a music and poetry concert.

I called the concert, Hawk From A Handsaw. The title came from a poem by Ogden Nash called The Strange Case of the Wise Child, about a boy called Pendleton Birdsong who was so smart he could tell a hawk from a handsaw.

The concert was a great success. McGough and Henri were fantastic and were given a standing ovation. They read all their best poems. Everyone loved the poems and the poets. We applauded till our hands hurt.

I was particularly thrilled that I got to read one of my poems, S.O.B., about the use of a sub-orbital bomb by the Russians. It went down surprisingly well.

Back in Chesterton, the freshness of the Liverpool poets' free verse swept through my head and gave me new energy and enthusiasm for poetry. I put more time into organising the weekly poetry meeting, the Poetry Stew, at the Dog and Duck pub on Bath Street.

Not everyone appreciated the tone of my poems, particularly one in which I talked about lusting after a beautiful girl.

"I've loved you three times already,

and you've only just walked in."

The landlord at the Dog and Duck took offence and banned the poetry group from holding our meeting there.

"I can't have you talking like that in my pub," he said. "You're upsetting my regulars. They don't want to hear about sex and stuff. They think you're a bunch of perverts and weirdos."

Our ejection from the pub made headlines. Pornographic Poem Row. Poetry club frozen out of pub, screamed the Derby Telegraph. It was a fun story, humorously written by my reporter friend, Peter Thompson.

It didn't change anything. It was the end of the poetry nights, but it wasn't the end of my career as an organiser of poetry and music events.

I got back in contact with McGough and Henri and a few other poets and musicians from Liverpool and hired them all to come to Chesterton to do a couple of concerts, one in the town hall and another at the college.

They came. Both events were a great success. Both events were sold out. Roger and Adrian hung out with us all in the pub, telling stories, sharing ideas, and recounting their adventures in Liverpool. They seemed to know the Beatles, especially Paul McCartney and John Lennon.

The thrill was also the feeling that Chesterton had become a little less provincial. For a moment, I felt like we were at the centre of something unique, creative, exciting and original.

It helped, of course, that I had friends like Rory and Peter to write stories in the Derby Telegraph and Nottingham Post publicising the concerts. They were glad to do it and always dashed off the stories without hesitation. They made me sound like the town's star impresario and cultural ambassador. I liked it.

The Messenger, on the other hand, was less than enthusiastic about my activities. Ron, my editor, couldn't have cared less.

"I think you're a bunch of weirdos," he said. "Why are you bringing these strange people from Liverpool here? I don't get it."

The Messenger refused to give me the resounding endorsement I wanted. On the contrary, it ignored everything I was doing and gave my concerts minimal publicity. I felt hurt at the time, but I was having far too much fun to really care.

It was around that time that I ordered two handmade suits, one pink and one yellow, specifically to wear at poetry and music events. The suits also did not go down well with the people in my office.

"What the hell are you wearing?" said Mrs Partridge.

"Oh my God, he's become a poofter," said Brenda.

"No, no, it's just a bright suit for my poetry concerts," I protested, but they were having none of it. They laughed and joked every time I walked in wearing one of the suits.

After the concerts, I got rid of them. I was getting too much ribbing as I walked through the town. I dumped the suits in the bin at the Goodwill shop. I never saw anyone wearing them. I assumed they went to a good home.

Rory came to all the music concerts and poetry readings. We spent a lot of time together doing pub crawls, going from one pub to another, from The Harrow to The White Horse to The Royal Oak to The Cottage. We had a preferred route.

Thursday nights were the best time for a crawl, as that was the night all the hen parties were also circulating through the pubs. Brides-to-be and their bridesmaids would be out in large groups, sweeping from one pub to another, getting more and more drunk as they went.

My work routine became as regular as clockwork. I

continued covering council and committee meetings at the town hall every Tuesday.

With time to spare, I would often pop into the La Scala cinema to catch whatever film was playing. This was how I got my first taste of Clint Eastwood's spaghetti westerns, The Good, the Bad and the Ugly and For a Few Dollars More. The problem was I never had time to see the whole film, so I always ended up going back and playing to see how it ended.

In those days, I went everywhere in Mo, my little Morris Minor. Sadly, that was to change.

One Friday morning, after I had delivered free papers to the police station, town hall and library, I was heading back to the office when a car pulled out in front of me. We collided head-on.

There was an awful sound of glass breaking and metal crunching. Mo was broken and bent with one wheel hanging off, steam pouring out of the radiator, and the bumper sent flying across the road.

"I'm so sorry," the other driver said. "I thought you were turning right."

"I was not turning at all. You drove into me!" I yelled. I felt like crying when I saw Mo all broken and smashed.

Still in shock, I picked up the rim of a headlight. I don't know why I did that. In a zombie-like state, I walked to the insurance office, but the agent told me there was nothing that could be done. Mo was too old to be fixed.

"It's what we call a write-off," said the agent. "All your car is fit for now is the dump."

Mo was towed to the junkyard. I watched through the fence as it was dropped into a pit with other smashed cars. It was one of the saddest days of my life.

After that, I went back to walking everywhere and taking the bus. It was a long time before I could afford to buy another car. Farewell, Mo. I will never forget you.

Rory came to help me drown my sorrows at the pub. I mused about organising a really big music and poetry concert.

"Why not make it free?" he said. "A free concert for the town to celebrate summer. You can get the council to sponsor you," he said. "You could invite the mayor, Mrs Vincent, and other dignitaries."

"Why don't I invite the Queen?" I joked.

"That's a good idea," said Rory. "You should invite the Queen. She likes music and poetry. Why not ask her?"

"Okay, I will. I'll write to Buckingham Palace and invite the Queen. Who knows, she might come."

"I think you're on to something," said Rory, and we clinked our beer glasses and laughed.

I set a date for the free concert. I decided to stage it in Victoria Park. I asked the council to sponsor it, and I went around asking all the town's shopkeepers and landlords to chip in to cover the cost.

"It's going to be a free concert for the whole town, a fun event for the whole family, in the park, on a sunny Sunday," I said. Reluctantly, they gave me donations. I didn't need much to cover the costs.

Meanwhile, I wrote a story about how awfully it was for coal miners to have to stand in the pouring rain, waiting for the bus to take them to the colliery.

I got a photo taken of them standing, getting soaking wet, waiting for the bus.

The story touched a nerve. There was an instant outpouring of sympathy. The council immediately dispatched a work crew to erect a spanking new metal and glass bus shelter for the miners.

The Messenger gave me credit. For a moment, I was a local hero. I considered it the most important piece of journalism I had ever done. It felt like a major accomplishment.

Plans for the free concert moved forward. More people offered support. Then, I got a reply from Buckingham Palace.

The Queen said she was delighted to be invited to the concert but, unfortunately, had other commitments that day.

"This letter comes to you with the warmest good wishes," Her Majesty wrote.

Rory phoned Buckingham Palace, and they told him that the letter's writing and signature indicated that the Queen had not only seen it but had probably handled it.

I was delighted. Rory and Peter wrote stories for their papers. The headlines said, "Queen tells poet: 'Sorry I can't come' and "Queen regrets she can't attend concert". I loved it.

* * *

CHAPTER THIRTY-NINE
FAREWELL

Sunday, June 24, 1972.

I looked out the kitchen window of my little terraced house, and it was pouring rain. Torrential rain. Not light, spitting, drizzly rain, but heavy, cats-and-dogs, soak-you-to-the-skin rain.

It was the day of the free poetry and music concert I had organised to be held in Victoria Park. This was a big deal as far as I was concerned. I had spent a lot of time planning and organising it, getting council approval, and raising money to pay for it. The last thing I wanted was for rotten weather to spoil everything.

All week, I had been praying for sunshine and blue skies. I wanted a bright, warm, sunny day with flowers in bloom, lawns freshly cut and a gentle breeze blowing through the tops of trees. I wanted everything to be perfect.

I looked at the sky. It was not blue, but dark and grey with menacing clouds pelting down enough water to fill a river.

In the park, council workers swept water off the stage of the bandstand while others pulled bunting out of boxes to string along railings and around columns.

My mind went back to the moment at the town hall when the

mayor, as chairman of the Estates Committee, gave me two thumbs in response to my application to use the bandstand in the park for a free concert.

Mayor Beatty had read out my application for the committee to consider.

"The concert will provide free entertainment for the people of Chesterton. It will be a fun day of poetry and music for everyone: families, working people, boys and girls, all the people of the town," it read.

Councillor Maggie Vincent was the first to endorse the idea.

"What a wonderful idea. I'm giving this my wholehearted support. And I fully intend to be there with my family and friends."

Not to be outdone, the mayor added his support.

"We need to make better use of Victoria Park, and this is an excellent way to bring people together for a fun time on a summer's day. I'm all for it."

The words were still ringing in my ears as I looked once again out the window to see if the rain had stopped. It hadn't. It was still coming down in buckets.

I had sent the Queen an invitation. Now I was glad she had said she turned me down and said she couldn't make it.

I imagined her walking unhappily on the park's great lawn, stepping through puddles on the wet grass while courtiers pranced around trying to hold a brolly over her head.

"Oh no," I thought, tortured by the image, "that would never do. What a disaster."

I had booked a Caribbean steel drum band. The music of The Jamaican All Stars was utterly infectious, impossible not to dance to. I had told people that trying to resist the urge to dance to the All Stars was like trying to take a shower without getting wet.

As I watched the rain coming down, I thought dancing to steel drum music today in the park would be just like taking a shower. You'd definitely get soaked. But I had not counted on the changeability of the English climate.

By midday, everything had changed. The clouds were gone. The sky was blue. The sun came out, dried up all the rain, and everything was suddenly sunny and bright, warm and delightful.

I arrived at the park just in time to catch the All Stars setting up their drums. They were laughing and joking and made no mention of the torrential downpour that had threatened to ruin everything an hour before. As far as they were concerned, we were in for nothing but sunshine and good times. I loved their carefree attitude.

Next to arrive was the young people's choir from the local Baptist church. They loved to sing upbeat pop songs like My Sweet Lord and Oh Happy Day.

The happy, sing-along, clap-along choir came dressed in colourful tie-dye T-shirts. Their music was modern and positive, suitable for all ages, with its emphasis on love, peace, and happiness. It was the perfect fit for a Sunday afternoon in the park.

Slowly, more and more artists turned up. Poets with words on paper and books to sell. Folk singers with acoustic guitars and serious songs to sing. I knew them all from past concerts. I had told them all to focus on love, peace and togetherness.

By 2 o'clock, a large crowd had gathered, walking in from all directions to find a spot on the grass around the bandstand.

The Allbrights came with friends and members of their church. Dylan Bishop came with his teacher friends from the Steiner school and a bunch of kids. They grabbed the best spot in front of the bandstand and put down large colourful picnic blankets.

The mayor and councillor Maggie Vincent arrived with family and friends and other members of the council. I greeted as many of them as I could with a smile and a hug or a handshake.

Annie turned up with her art college pals and her new boyfriend. She introduced him as a lover of Gauguin and a gifted water-colourist. He smiled at me as if he had known me for years.

Rory came with Peter and Garry from the Telegraph. We laughed about what they would write. They said they would write whatever I wanted them to write.

"Names sell papers," I said. "Write down as many names as you can."

Lurking in the shade of chestnut trees, I spotted the Messenger staff, Ron, with his wife, Patricia, and Brenda, with her mom, Pat, and cousins, Sophie and Maureen. Harold Watson came with his wife, Mildred, and Mrs. Partridge came alone. I didn't give any of them a hug. I waved and smiled, and they all waved and smiled back.

The All Stars got things off and running with their delightful, energetic, sunny Caribbean steel drum music.

It was a gloriously upbeat, happy-go-lucky start. People immediately got up and danced. The Steiner people danced with everyone, pulling strangers up from the grass to join the dancing.

I looked around the park, and people were having a good time, talking, laughing, and having picnics. It was just as I had hoped it would be. Fun and friendly, happy and safe. It was a joyful, colourful scene with people dressed in their summer finery.

There were young girls in pretty summer dresses dancing with young men wearing white pants and striped boating jackets, as if they were about to go for a boat ride on the river.

The atmosphere was calm, gentile and respectable, like a private garden party. I imagined the Queen passing out cream cheese and cucumber sandwiches. The thought made me smile.

People I had written about over the years came up to say hello and to thank me for putting on the concert. Sam Small, the pigeon fancier, came up and told me he didn't care for poetry or folk music, but he wanted to see the flowers in the park.

When the last song had been sung and the last poem read, I thanked everyone for coming. Ron came and shook my hand. Councillor Boyd gave me a hug. Rory saw and looked jealous.

People started to drift away, disappearing into the park. The All Stars packed up their drums. The musicians were as cheerful at the end as they were at the beginning. They were all smiles and laughter as they waved goodbye. I watched them go and waved and waved until their little van bounced down the street and vanished around the corner.

After the excitement of the concert, life in the office felt rather dull and boring. Harold gave us all a scare when he started wearing shorts because it was summer. Mrs Partridges told him, "Shorts are for wearing at the beach, not in the office", but he didn't stop.

Mrs Partridge and Brenda decided to go on holiday together to France. It was an idea they had been talking about for a long time. Brenda was excited and insisted on practising her French on everyone, much to the annoyance of Mr Watson.

My exam result came in from the college in Preston. I had passed all three levels on my first attempt, which was unusual. Most people pass one or two parts but never all three. I was delighted. It felt like quite a feather in my cap, but no one cared.

It was at that moment that I decided it was time for me to move on, leave the Messenger, and find a new job.

I had enjoyed four wonderful years in Chesterton. I felt like a native son. I knew all the shopkeepers. I knew all the councillors. I knew everyone at the library, the co-op, the police station, and the post office. I knew everyone in the town hall. It was normal for me to walk through the town saying hello to pretty much everyone on the street. As I say, it was a small town.

I knew every street. I knew the shortcuts, the posh areas, and the poor areas, all the school, churches and pubs.

I had a serious sense of the rhythm of the town. I felt that I could take its pulse and tell you its heart rate.

Sometimes, I thought my time in Chesterton was like going to a school for the first time. When you start, on day one, you know no one and all your surroundings feel strange, but after a few years, you end up knowing everyone, good, bad and forgettable, as well as every nook and cranny in the place.

With my diploma in my pocket, I applied for a new job, a better job at a bigger newspaper, a city paper with a much larger circulation.

I sat in my little terraced house and typed letters of application to a few big city papers. I ended up typing the letters a few times because I kept making mistakes. I got a reply from the paper in Bristol within a few days, offering me a job.

Leaving the Messenger was not as sad as I thought it would be. It felt like the time was right. It was the most natural thing to do.

Few words were spoken. There were no hugs or kisses, no long speeches, no tearful goodbyes. I got a handshake from Ron and Harold. They wished me well. Brenda and Mrs Partridge were still on holiday in France, so I never got to say goodbye.

My last sight of the office was as I waited for the bus to Nottingham, the same bus that brought me to Chesterton four years earlier.

I climbed the stairs to the top deck and looked back at the office as the bus moved slowly away, up the hill I had run down all those years ago.

The office got smaller and smaller until it disappeared completely from view. My time in Chesterton was done and dusted.

* * *

Manufactured by Amazon.ca
Bolton, ON